# LEARN NODE-RED IOT PROJECTS WITH ESP32

## MQTT, ESP32-Cam, Machine Learning Node, RFID, TLS and More Projects

By

Jazlyn Selvi

# TABLE OF CONTENTS

3

# WHY DOCKER

We're going to discuss why Docker is so common and why you should use Docker instead of a traditional installation way. First of all, I have here patina on bits and software, we will also install the later that you where you can see all the installation from the micro services. And one of the main thing is that every container and every image is really isolated on the system. That means if I'm click here to stop or kill, then all of the data from not read will be vanished from my operating system. And that's really a good and common way to keep your operating system clean. But Docker is much more. It also means for example, if I'm installing WordPress, some good example, WordPress has some database has some web server on it. And of course, the blood or the WordPress itself. So mainly three dependencies. When you're using Docker, for WordPress, all of the dependencies will be installed inside the Docker container. And this is really a good way how you can fast install and software on a system. The next really good point is that you can roll out all of your software with one command. That means I testing my system with Docker on a testing operating system on a testing server. And then with one Docker command, I can implement all of my software inside another server, it's for backup routines, and also gives us much more consistently and possibility. And that's what we want nowadays. It's also very efficient.

So let me see if I can find here and good image because Docker will directly access the Linux, the Linux kernel. So instead of a virtualization where the capacity from the PC or the virtual machine takes a lot of resources, Docker, not is not acting like an virtual machine. But it's really accessing the and Linux Linux kernel. And this is also what we want. So it's flexibility, rapid development, it's really efficient, it's isolated, and we have inconsistency and portability. So overall, Docker provides and convenient and in my way and my opinion and efficient way to manage and deploy application. And which has made it an increasingly popular choice for developers and also for IT professionals. And this is what also is used in the private sector. And as you can see here, we can install here, everything on Docker. This is the host OS and this is the hardware. And that's why on Container Engine is really fast. Of course and virtual machine is also fast. But with these Docker engines, we have a lot of flexibility.

# GET A VSERVER

I would like to create an IF WE server with Hetzner. Hetzner is one of the cloud providers, which has server locations in Germany, in Finland and in the US, and the prices for the service are really good. And the good thing is, they calculate it on an hourly basis, that means that I now can create and show you the server, I have a test environment. And later on, for example, after three hours, I can delete everything and only pay for the three hours. And the monthly rates are very good. So when we go in here to the prices of the cloud servers, we can see, we have here for example, I would say at a minimum, two cores, four gigs of RAM, 40 gigs of disk space traffic, you have 20 terabytes IP for five form. And you can choose the locations. Germany, Finland, and also here, the United States, NT will pay for roundabout, this is in Euro, roundabout for four to $5 at an average of $5.05 to $6 for this option, and as you can see, also the hourly rate is really good. And therefore I would say it's absolutely and very good price. But there are also other companies as well, like Digital Ocean, etc. Just use one where you have access and server images. So that we can choose here what we want. Now we're going back. And I would like to show you how easy it is to do that. And also in the links of this server, you'll get an link for Hetzner that you get 20 euros as an gift when you are register to the Hetzner cloud server. So now let's start with we adding here and server.

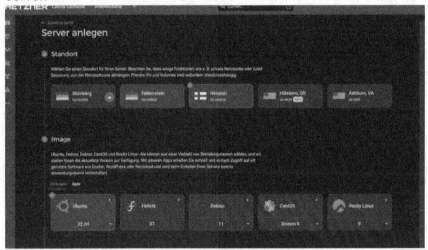

And basic thing is that we are choosing here our location. And in my case, I would like to have here in Germany in German standard location, then I'm choosing Ubuntu. And as you can see here, the main disk operating systems are you can choose also you can choose here some apps if you would like to have but open to is the best one. And now just for training purpose, I choose the cheapest one because we just want to install it and later on I have another test server. And that's it. You can upload your your SSH key, but I would like to do it with the normal root passwords. Yeah, you can change the name and then on the right, you can say okay, now I would like to buy it. And to create it, we click on creation. And that's it. Now I've got an email with the root password. And here is the IP address. So we can now open our terminal and then we say SSH root then I have to see where's my passwords then let's see, yes, the fingerprint is okay. Then the passwords then we change the passwords and, as always, I've entered not the new ones or current passwords. New one, new one does not match. Next Next try so once again and again. And now we are on our machine that means for example the CD use local SPN and here we are creating later on our our files are for the Docker components. That's it. That's what we want to have our V server on the internet so that we can choose here and proper location for a smartphone and be aware when you have an online virtual machine running you are responsible for every security issues. So and also to keep the machine up to date. And that means always using strong password and we go through it later on because I A lot of scripts will try to enter your server and therefore choose and really good password and also use fail to benefit. Keep and keep the firewall open and steady, closed I mean, so that the server will have the best security as possible.

# DOCKER INSTALLATION

We want to install Docker and therefore we are using the official Docker documentation engine installed Ubuntu. And now we're going through all of the bash commands so that we can install here, Docker on the system. First of all, we should update our machine and also get here the CA certificates curl, and those two programs. So let's copy and paste it in and let the magic happen. afterwards. When we have installed the first part, we are creating here in a new folder with EDC, apt key rings and also download the GPG codes. So let's do it. Copy and paste. That's it, you can paste it in the terminal with CTRL SHIFT and we always right click and paste it because the normal Ctrl C will just exit or interfere with the last comment. Then here is the GPG key and copy paste. And this we already had this one use the following command to set up the repository that it then installed Docker engine, we have already updated it. So once again, because we did hear something in the background so that we can download everything. That's okay and then install Docker. See, that's the Community Edition be aware of the East Enterprise Edition.

This is an open source one, we want the command line allswell And also the plugins and the Docker compose plugin. So we're installing here, a few programs. So you can see 400 megabytes. Let's do it. And in the meantime, while this is installing, I would like to show you the Docker hub page Docker Hub is where all of the images are localized. And an image is I would say the main thing behind the Docker container and therefore we can search the Hello World. This gives you a good indication on is this an and trustworthy source or not. As you can see 1 billion downloads is the official Docker image from hello world. And hello world means that this will show you if the container and Docker is set up in the right way. And this is exactly what we want to do now. So therefore, we are trying to hear docker run hello world. And often it's so that we we don't let's take a look, we have to use sudo it's so that when we are using a docker run command, then the image is on the server already downloaded. But when the docker run sees a ha the hello world is not there, then it will be pulled and pull means download the image and afterwards it's could could be run but the run has all also the pull command implemented so therefore I haven't downloaded the HelloWorld image. I say now sudo docker run hello world. And it you see unable to find the image and the image will be downloaded. And now we see status downloaded new new image this is the latest one. And now we see hello world from Dhaka and this message shows that your installation appears to be working correctly. And

11

this is exactly what we tried to do. And the first test shows us we are ready to go with Docker on our Ubuntu system.

# RUN MOSQUITTO IN THE CONTAINER

And now I would like to test if the mosquito container is working properly. And therefore, we want to enter the container so that we have access of the mosquito commands. And we How could we enter and Kadena. So with docker ps, for example, we see Aha, these containers are running, or you can see it here he is the name. And I would like to have your mosquito server, that's the name. If you have here some strange names, then you have missed the tech minus minus name. And it will be assigned from patina or from Dhaka in a random way. But here, the mosquito server, this is our desired location. Therefore, Docker exec, because we want to enter an interactive mode. That's the reason why I give on this parameter, then the name, it's called mosquito server. And at the end, I would like to have here, the bash, and our I'm inside here, the mosquito serve our container. And you see here's a little file system from inline Linux system.

And that's exactly what we have here. So we can enter here also, for example, the mosquito, and here you can see the config data and lock. This is what we entered here. Here, we say please enter in the config and when we see the config. And then we could say here cut mosquito dot config, you can see here, the thing what we entered before is now inside the container. So but what I want to do here is I have access here on the normal mosquito command line commands. And the first thing is we for example, help you help is that what I want to see him mosquito Publish. And you can see here I have the command that I can send an M Quiddity message directly from the command line. And don't be puzzled. We are discussing these things later on much more in detail. I just want to test if the Docker container runs correctly and as I could see here, the mosquito command works so let's test it out with mosquito pup to publish ah is where we want to have the server it's of course localhost and the topic will be test and just a message and we got no error. So this seems to be working correctly. And with this example I would like to show you how you can enter here and container directly from your system and with exit with jumping back out of to our operating system. And we are here in the mosquito folder.

# OHMYZ FOR MORE CONVENIENT TERMINAL HANDLING

And therefore we say apt install, said, S H, that's the first thing what we need. And then I would like to install all my dish. And all my Tish is an, I would say, an command line tool for its gifts your most structure, it's a better overview and therefore all my dish and we go in here down to the installation part, we copy this one, paste it in.

And now the Armitage will be installed, do you want to change the default shell to to this Ah, yes, I would like to have it. And now you can see it's much more cleaner. And what I have also here in communist for example, I'm typing in a now an M and clicking on the tablet one, you see yours some reference what I could do. So when I want to change it to mosquito, I just have to type in CD then an M tableta. And there is only one possible solution for his commands. Therefore, there is no suggestion it will will make here and how to fill and I can jump here into this one. And I don't have here all of the long M commands where I be here because with

PVD I can see this is my location and I don't need it here in the full way gives us a more structured way to work on the terminal.

# NODE-RED

Next step is to install Node red, therefore, we are creating a new folder, it's called node red. And the first thing what we are doing now is we are creating here and volume, Docker volume, create node red data. And also, what we want to do is we want to change here. Not now we want to create also, you know, the Reds node red data, that's what we want, so that we have here our data file in it. And now, I would like to change the owner, once again, recursively for everything to the user 1000. So when we are seeing here, the owner is your node read 1000. Then I jump into the folder. Once again, let's see. And also the node read data has here in folder with 1000. Yeah, and you're on the node read the docs, we can see that we have here a new volume, what we are just created here. And we are saving the data to not read the data. But not with two underlines, I created just one underline and here will be stored the data into directly data. And that's all what we need in the docker run command. I've created my own version. So let's see what we have here.

15

And copy. Now let's paste it. So docker run in the background, the port is 1880. And here we have the folder for our volume, the name is no dread the restart policy. And we have here, of course, also, the latest image, a bol if you're not having an volume, all of your data will be vanished if the server is restarting, or if we want will kill the container, for example, that's absolutely necessary that you have here and persistent data. So let's see. And also, let's check node ready starting it takes a few seconds that the container is established, we can type in the pot and wait a few seconds. And here we go. We have our note read. If you mixed your something up with the volume, there will be an info we windows. So let's see how we can do that I will show you, for example. We are using the last statement here without on volume. Or you mix something up, then refresh it needs a few seconds. And then you get here and warning. And this warning says to you please check if you have started this container with the volume to slash data. Otherwise, any flow changes are lost when the redeploy or upgrade the container. That's absolutely mandatory. So once again, I'm removing the container up up with where do we have it? Yep, so once again, we creating the container. And now we should have the container with the proper file in it. And we can here save it. And the persistent data is now let's see here. Node read data. Everything is in here. So this load dot JSON when I'm now printing out flow JSON, then we have here the flow one. We have here, the inject node with the timestamp and if I'm changing here for example, to string let me see if I can find you. Then we click here on deploying. Cut flow and then let me see if you can find the URL. Then that means we can back up the flow stop chasing inside the node read data and we have a backup of all of our stuff from node read.

# NODE-RED WITH AUTHENTICATION

And as we did before, we also want to secure our node red with some password identification, because otherwise, it will also be accessible for everyone. And that's not what we want. Therefore, we also using the existing container that we are making your password out of it. It's also documented in the official documentation. Therefore, we say Docker exec it node red, that's the name of the container as H for the bash, and it's called now NP x node red admin hash. PW now we have to adhere and passwords, let's make this the same as we had before. So, we copy this one and now we could exit. So, now we have saved the password. So on to now we are inside the node read data. So be aware where we are doing this. So inside the node read data, we have here the settings Yat s, j, s, and we are adding now this file. But this file is inside the container we have then copied to our persistent data because otherwise, this will be overwritten each time.

17

But we need here the files inside therefore, nano settings J S, then with control and W we can search for auth once again, and here we have the authentication. It's uncomment. It commented and here we uncomment everything and be aware here also from the spaces because it's an Yamo data on JSON data. Therefore, we have to keep here exactly the spaces. So admin auth credentials, here, you can use change the username, but what we want to do is change the password hash. Also with the.at the end then we are pasting in our value Ctrl X Yes, Enter. And now we have to copy the settings. JS to our persistent folder. And I would say we are jumping back to this folder and this is where I want to have the JSON data. Therefore I say CP for copy node ratted data settings, JS should be copied here with setting GS There we go. Or let's say 10 seconds GS. Without do I have written it right, I think I have last year and so setting GS should be called settings. Jas, once again to settings. Now it works okay, perfectly. Now we have here our file settings je s with the authentication part. And now we are jumping to our patina, killing the node red and remove it, just remove it, get rid of it. And now we have the perfect example because now we deleted the container and have one inject note here. So when we are pulling out and creating the new container, this should be here, because it's saved here in the persistent data.

But before we run the command for the node read, we have to add here something and this is this volume, the settings J S should be linked and mounted to data settings J S, because in the persistent data it won't be overwritten. And also I'm adding here an environment variable. It's called for Europe puzzles so that I have the same time zone as the server has, for example. Then let's start it again. Let's see if the container is already started. Once again, refresh it. And now we have here an outer deification prompt, I think have edit here the admin then my passwords not the hash that are wrecked password. And there we go. And as you can see, although we have deleted and removed the previous container, the content is now here because we have our float chasen in not read data folder. And here we go.

# INFLUXDB

The next step is that we are installing influx dB. And influx DB is an open source time series database for recording metrics, events and analytics. And we will use it later on for saving the temperature values. For example, from sensors or also the power voltage data from Shelleys entered us motor devices, therefore rechecked Of course, everything here, we creating an new folder in on our server on influx dB. To get more information about influx dB, this are really an good documentation of what is all about, and how does it work. And we are using the influx DB tool. First of all, always dark mode. And there you can see the queries etc. Really, really a lot to do. In your self study, for example, here, we want to focusing on installing the influx dB. Therefore we create at the very first beginning as always in volume, influx dB. And then we could start with the docker run command, the docker run looks like the following. I would like to have it on port 8086.

This is the persistent data. It's the following path with influx DB and this VAR lib influx DB tune. I have it from the net. Let's see here from the documentation. Here you are. And the name is in flux DB restart policy in flux DB latest. That's it. So let's pull the image and then switching here to my container list. Now it should be here in flux dB. Let's see if there's any error in the locks. A lot of stuff, no error so far. Then instead of node red, we are typing in 8086. And yes, welcome to influx dB. Is that isn't that easy and really easy to get started. Here we are typing in our username. And be aware we have to add something else then our passwords then the initial organization name, we need these two variables later on. So I call it also pixel Eddie and the initial bucket. I call it no dread because everything what I'm getting to node red, I will put into the bucket name, node red and bucket name is like and database and table. So when we click on continue, we are here in influx dB. And then we saying Quickstart. And on the left side you see here for example, the buckets, you can add some buckets, that means more databases. And here under sources. You also see which clients it's really amazing. You just can click on Arduino for example. And you can add here on UTC and here the code where you can access InfluxDB directly from an Arduino USB, but we want to have it over no dread with em Quiddity. But maybe you have here some other circumstances where you can use it also CSGO for example, you can save your data directly. Absolutely amazing. So but I would like to show you also here and members. Nope. About you consider organization organizational profile user ID and organization ID because this is what we are also needing later on. And we are needing the API tokens.

# GRAFANA

And as easy as we install in flux to be, we are installing Grafana Grafana is an dashboard, where we can easily visualize a lot of data. And you can see here, for example, such dashboards are by drag and drop are made, and the data sources in flux dB. So those two components work perfectly together. And how can we install it, as of course, just one docker run command, and we are ready to go. But before we have to change, here, again, the directory, so we're creating here Cavanna, then jumping into Grafana, then we are making a new volume. And we are starting here with Grafana. There's not really anything to back up, therefore, you can add here and volume, I'm skipping that part because I'm not really picking up here, my dashboards, if it got lost, okay, then I have to make it again, or I can export it. But this is not nothing what I really need on a daily basis, therefore, I'm skipping this part.

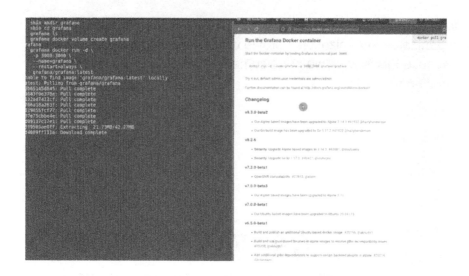

But if you want to, then you have the volume. And you can see in the Docker image where you can add here, the volume. So I'm installing on the port 3000. And be aware a lot of other containers are running on 3000. If you have V or something else, then you put on the first 3000 For example 3001, etcetera, then you could change it. So then should be running. Let's see. Here we have our Grafana take a look on the locks. Also here, I think there is no error. And here we go. Here we are in Grafana and Grafana takes an audit approach. So that means that we have here some standard logins and this is admin, admin, and now we have a new password no dread coos tastic 2023 And there we go, we are inside Grafana and later on, we are creating yours some dashboards but before we have to add to the data sources, and you also can add my MySQL Maria dB.

# MARIADB AND CREATE A DB VIA CLI

I'm sure all of you knows my SQL. It's an SQL database, and the fork of MySQL is Maria dB. So it's the same, nearly the same engine behind it. So you can use nearly the same. Let's see if there is some good overview. And why is there a fork because MySQL, the company is overtaken by another company. And the community thought this is not really an open source project anymore, and therefore there was an fork, it's called Maria dB. And of course, you can use MySQL. But in this scenario, I would like to introduce you to Maria dB. And in the official document, you see how you can install it on Docker.

And of course, also in the Docker Hub, you can see 1 billion downloads, how you can install it with Docker, it's very easy. We just go into a new folder, Maria dB. And then let's see what we have here. For example. The name here we have an password. And of course, you're also the image as well, I already have prepared some code, then we pasting in it, I will leave the standard port at 3306. The name is MDB for Maria dB, the Maria DB password, I change it. It's every time the same in this course. And the latest image user is the standard route in this case. And now we let the program the container be installed. So let's refresh it. There we go. And later on, we also take a closer look at minor. That's an graphic interface for managing the database. But I would like to show you how you can also add here are some databases in sight on container. Therefore, it's the same procedure as we did in the mosquito case and in the node rats case. So we say Docker, exec idea. And then MDM MTB is the name of the container, then it's called Maria DB or MySQL, it depends on the image what you're using. And then we are seeing a user with dash dash, then root, and then the PII for the password without any space, then it will be entered directly. And this is no red cause 2023 Welcome to Maria DB monitor. So now I can create your database. For example, create database, node, read, costs, semicolon, enter, and we have created our database. And we will see this database later on, I can go out of it with exit. And now I'm here already in my folder. That's it. That's all what we need. And I'm not creating any volume there. Why is that so because normally, you're backing up an SQL database was an SQL dump. And you have perfectly you can perfectly use now these Docker Docker exec commands and can fetch your an SQL statement and put an SQL statement so that you get an SQL dump and this SQL dump you will be backing up and not the engine by itself.

# ADMINER

Maybe some of you knows PHP my admin but it minor is much more reduced to the basics and works very well when you have installed and Maria DB database directly on your system, you just only need one single php file to edit your whole your whole database. So let's see an online demo. It's really reduced as you can see, but you can everything do what we want to do, you can create databases we can implement SQL commands important export things. So let's see how can we do that we also have here and Docker container Why is that so because we need to also and web server etc. In the normal case, and with this minor Docker container, everything is ready to go. Therefore, you can see the Docker command docker run link.

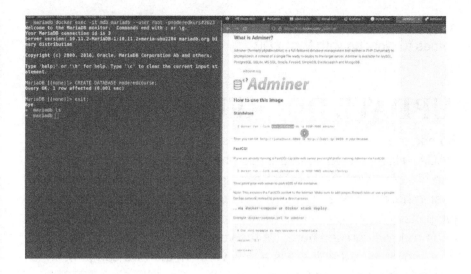

And here we have to link our database so that the container knows what is here going on. And that's it. So we don't really need here some extra folder dev for Docker run D for the background link MD BM that's my Maria database name from the container then it's linked to the DBM I would like to have the port 80 ATM name is it minor restart always add minor latest and go for it. And as you can see, the whole Docker infrastructure will grow and grow but it doesn't take too much space so far. So let's test that minor here I copy and paste IP and then we enter here at atm and now we want to have MySQL it's okay the server is now empty beer we can add here directly I'm not sure let's test it if we have to add the IP or we can add the container name but let's switch to English MDB username is root and of course normally you should add here some username inside the Maria DB and that you can do later on and now I have an user and password in order to cause hashtag 2023 and now I'm in my Maria DB database and as you can see here is the node red course what we are created before here and inside the node red course of course there are no any no tables so far we could create the end table we can add your SQL commands and also create import export everything what we need and also when we are creating new something. So let's see that it was to, to fasts once again. For example here, all plugins select data until we have also the possibility to see what is going on in the table and can modify it can change it can delete it really handy. Must have when it comes to working with Maria DB

# UPDATE DOCKER CONTAINER

So one major question maybe comes to your mind when it comes to DACA? How can we update those programs. And this is an easy one. So I'm switching here, for example to read. And what we're seeing here is this is our current version of node red. Let's also jump insights. Where do we have it for example here insight from node red, we can see here, it's the version 3.0. Point two. And if you now knows, now that there is a new version, then we can jump in to Docker Hub. Node red for example.

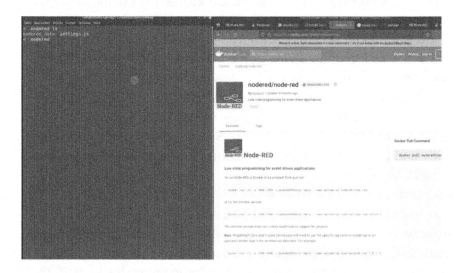

And we could there, pull it. So that means we have an image, Docker pull node red, node red, Enter. And now the latest image will be downloaded to your server in this case, image is up to date, but otherwise it will be updated. And then we can go a year and say, for example.com, stop node red. Then we are deleting the existing node read the container, then we can say of course, Docker container, prune that we are deleting everything. And now we're just starting with our docker run command. Node red again. And now the newest image will be used. And as we can see, all of our data should be persistent. Let's see. Although if we have really deleted your the container, of course you can do it also with patina. We have here the actual version, the up to date version, and this is how you can do it with the Docker things. And of course, you can write your own bash scripts, for example, read all of the images what you have on your Docker, then automatically with a follow for example, loop through it, pull it and then just create the new Docker runs.

# TRAEFIK AS REVERSE PROXY FOR SSL ACCESS

In this chapter now is for everyone who wants to dig a little bit deeper into the Docker world and also into the network world. Traffic is a reverse proxy. And there are different kinds of reverse proxy. It's also H A proxy and also nginx has an reverse proxy as well. And the reverse proxy is that we have here from the World Wide Web, the really the bad internet. And we have here and subdomain and this subdomain will be directed to traffic on the port, for example, 443. And this is encrypted via SSL. This is on our server and behind our server, this is unencrypted. And traffic will direct it there. According to the domain. To our microservices. This means when I'm calling here, node, red dots domain.com, traffic will direct it to the port 1880. But in the front end, it's everything is decrypt, encrypted. And here, it's directed directly onto the server. If I'm connecting here, for example, portainer, then the boat 9000 will be attached. And this is what we want to install now.

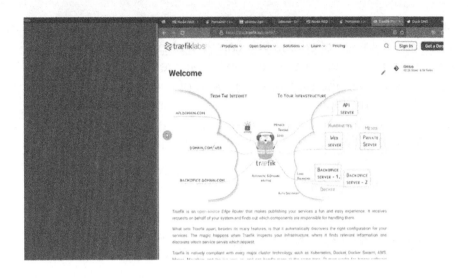

And also that we access traffic directly via SSL. And therefore, there, of course, is nearly an a whole chapter, how we could set up traffic, this is just a fast purpose. And if you have any question, you need a little bit more time to research a few things because I have to assume that you know a few points, what is an SSL certificate what is Let's Encrypt etcetera. But stay with me. And we make here everything together. So first of all, we need an subdomain. So if you have already a domain, you can create an subdomain. Or if you want a free version, you could use any kind of doing DNS service there are a lot of different Indian so as I'm using duck DNS, I have here five different slots for for me frame. Therefore I'm taking here my new IP address. And I see for example, terrific Ubuntu on now I would like to have a new one, I would say here, terrific node read its domain. Terrific no dread cause there we go on, then I update here on the IPM. And now, traffic node red cause dot duck DNS dot orgy will not really work because it will direct me to the port 80 of my server and I haven't got any web server installed, etc. And also if I skip here to HTTPS, it doesn't work because the DNS service will need here some certificate but we created here the entry. This is one of the first step on our server we are creating here in a new folder called traffic. And inside traffic. We are creating here three new files what we are filling immediately. Then Docker Compose. We need traffic dot Yama and we need your traffic underlying API dot Yamo. That's what we need. So what is Docker Compose? In

28

the previous projects we use the docker run command that means we are directly typing in the fields in the Docker compose means in each folder, whereas in Docker compose we can now use Docker compose up for example, and then this file will be used and the Docker container will be created. So it's a more persistent way. Why I'm not using this for the whole course. Because somewhere you have to stop all of the content that is not overwhelming you on the docker run is an easy start. If you want to change your all of your Docker containers with Docker Compose, it's really easy afterwards to do it. So there is no Docker compose installed therefore we have to apt get Docker compose let's see. Get install Docker compose There we go. Then as the next point before We can enter here something into the Docker Compose, we have to add, I think a password. Now, let's enter your null Docker compose Yama, Enter, and copy and paste here from terrific from the documentation here inside. So what do we have this in younger fine. So be also be aware of the spaces, use the services until you can enter a name, how you would like to have, use the container name, restart policy unless stopped, always the image is terrific, then you have to create your network that's really unnecessary because later on, we also want to coordinate traffic, our node red instance, and therefore we have to adhere something. Then I have here the ports 80 and 44. Three, that's the unencrypted and with SSL, here we have the volume for TOCOM. And those two files, we just edit with touch. And the dot Acme JSON is where Let's Encrypt later on, we'll save the whole the whole files for our certificates, then we need to say external is true so that other Dockers can also container can also access these network. So when we are saving this one, and now let's see. So we are not creating it now, the Docker file because we need before the other files as well. So therefore, we are making an odd turn so that we get here and password. And we can do it with an HTTP and D image. And we say for example, admin node red cars, and this will be the excess data for traffic later on. So let's do it. One dash too much. Unable to find HTTP, D image, it will be downloaded. And here we go.

I have done let's see. Once again, a typo. So docker run RM httpd HDD password, I've forgotten it, then NBHM admin and node red coos, that's my password. So this is what I want here, copied. Also with this last dot, and now I have the password, then we have to add something in traffic API dot Yamame. And I copy paste the content. And don't forget here to change the password. What we just already created, therefore, was the cursor, I'm jumping back and then fill in the password. There we go. And we can save also dystrophic analyst API and this will be need for our authentification and be aware here we have to add our traffic node to read cause hosts with your terrific node red course, dot duck DNS also be aware he our other apprentices then in this line, then Save to buffer. Yes, the second file we have edited. So the last file should be there traffic dot Yamo file, also copy and pasted the thing in and what we have here, give me the entry points from our IoT network. It should be the 80 port and the web secure should be 44 screen. It should be the HTTPS. Also the API we have already insert dashboard should be true email. Yeah, we wants to have an incorrect email because because when Let's Encrypt, this is our certificate authentication, authentication, authentication, when we are getting an error, all the three months will be over and it's not any more valid, then we will notified on this address so this should be an we'll address. Here's our network IoT network and also from the API and

that the dashboard could be accessed here the link to this file, okay.
Also this file can be saved now.

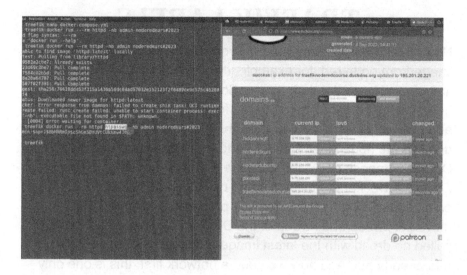

So now everything we put everything together then we are creating
the network.com net work, create Ibu D network. Very good. And
now we can say Docker compose up and also with the parameter d
that is runs in the background. And now pulling the traffic image.
And now we can see if everything works, right. So let's see in
patina, we should now have traffic. Let's see under the locks.
Loaded, terrific Yama file looks good. Now we can open the traffic
node red course dot stack DNS dot orgy. It's already refreshed. And
you see here is already in certificates or not. Let's see again, I'm
logging in here is admin and my password. Here we go. This is the
terrific dashboards. And now we are secure on we have verified
from Let's Encrypt. And this is often be shown with our tool for
example, let's show the certificate. And it's valid for three months on
this DNS entry.

# SSL FOR NODE-RED WITH TRAEFIK LABELS

Now I would like to show you how you can secure your Docker image from node red, for example, through the traffic. Therefore, first of all change the dark theme. So clear. Then what do we have here, I'm jumping into the node red folder. Then what we want to add here is, let's see, I keep everything inside but in the protein. I'm deleting the node Rhett's image. And we're creating here in a Docker compose dot Yamo because it's more convenient if we use it within a Docker compose file and not within docker run commands. Therefore, I've already prepared something with universal sweep and sweep of the Docker compose the service is called no dread with the latest image, the environment variable we had already put. And now we need a network first, this is one only for node red. And here we have the IoT network which listens also to our traffic, then yeah, the volume we could also then add in here the settings data but just for training purpose will leave its own until we have some labels. Area container which should be configured with traffic should have now those labels. First of all, we have in traffic and abled is true. Then, the service is called node red when we call it ASDF. For example, then we have to add here is the F, this name should be the same name as here.

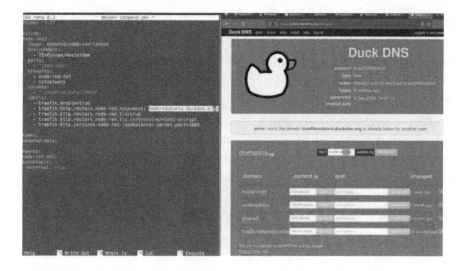

Then we have to add here some new hostname therefore I'm creating a new one. So node red, Ubuntu I delete this one, then I'm saying for example. We call it traffic node red. Let's see if it's available. It's not available graphic node red, cause that's exactly what we have here. Haha, then we terrific and node red is that available. That's a well around then adding the IP address. Then we copy this subdomain or the student DNS domain jumping with the cursor to the rights points and now we are entering here. traffic traffic node red duck DNS or Jeem, then we have TLS should be true TLS resolver is Let's Encrypt. And here, the load balancer should point to one point 8.0 Of course does have to be aligned with this one. So if we are adding then calling now this DNS, it's on port 443 traffic then now as a middleware redirects it to this port, okay. Docker minus compose up minus d. And so now let's see what container we haven't got edit here any name, but as you can see here, node red will be started and now without a password because we haven't referenced the settings, but it's you can do it in the same way as referenced before. Now let's see into the traffic. Here we have traffic node red course all the other hosts hosts and here we go traffic node red with a green sign that means we are on then, let's see if we have here success dot duck DNS, or GM. Here we go. Here we have our it's saved very good admin. And here we go. We have an secure, Let's Encrypt with and certificate are three, three months. And also after the three months traffic will renew the

33

files. And as you can see, everything is in it. And you can see here is the official DNS with the SSL. But you can of course also access it without an HTTP so be aware HTTPS And then the IP address with 1880. And then you can exit it directly. That's also possible but when you be on outside, of course, only use here some SSL decrypt encryption. Okay and in this matter in this with this labels, you can now add to all of your container in insecure way and also in a persistent way and because with this Docker Compose, you don't have to save your Docker run commands. And now you have a perfectly set up Docker network with all of your microservices and also with an SSL certificate.

# CRONJOBS FOR BACKUP ROUTINES

No Backup are no mercy. And this is another reason why I would like to introduce you to crontab. And also to cron jobs. cron jobs are in the Linux and Ubuntu world tasks that are scheduled to run automatically to a specific interval using the cron activity. So definitely, we can say, no, no, it is etc, Chrome tab. And here we have the ability to enter scripts, which will be scheduled on a fixed time. And the schematic is always the same. So here we have, for example, 12345 digits, the first digit is the minute, then we have the hour, the day, the month, and the day of the week. And now with these digits, we can say for example, let's jump here to the ends that for example, every day at two in the morning, 230 in the morning, as script should be executed. Or we could say every Monday or Okay, now it's Sunday through every Monday at 230.

This script should be executed, and so on, and so on. And what I did in this room, so that I can visualize how Uncrowned shop works is that every minute because you have to place order to start. Then we have the username, as you can see root. And this is now the commands, this could be an file and shell file or in this case, it's an command. I write into an file. This is what I'm right here are my first clones up. This is the Append print command into this file. This means every minutes, this will be executed so that this text will be appended into the crone t x t under the s bin. So let's see, I've already entered it, then ls wefew. The cron txt cut cron txt, and as you can see 123445 minutes can also see system control status. cron job, chrome tip is it is called just grown. So clear. System Status Chrome, and then you can see one when was the last time it was triggered? And it's triggered right away. So then now No, etc crontab. I get rid of them because I don't want to spam my system with this text file. And this is how we could execute some files via the crontab

# BACKUP OF NODE-RED FLOWS VIA CRONJOB

Let us now create some backup routine. Therefore, if you make the backup CD backup, then we are making an new file which is called backup.sh. Then s always at the beginning of such files, we need a shebang. And this is called bin bash. Then we say for example, you have variable and we say your dates. And I would like to have the current number of the dates because I would like to make it more dynamically backup dot JSON. So I want today we have here the 22 of March. And I would like to have the number 22. Because I want to make every day and backup so that I have always one month of backups. So next month, the 22 will be overwritten with the April content. And so I have nearly 30 to 31 backup standards each month and this is exactly what I want to have. So then we copy the file from node read the chasen file that's in the flows dot JSON we already have under have reviewed it therefore, this is under User local eSpin node read then we called our folder node read data and there is the flow stop chasing inside and we want to copy it in to use our local eSpin backup and then we add here the day. I think this should work.

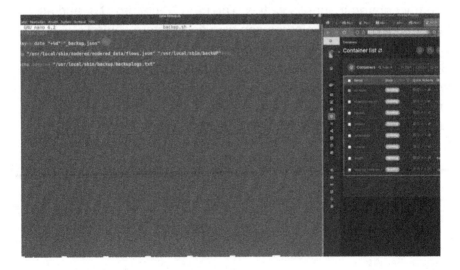

So let's do a little bit in decides then in the next room, we make also and txt file so that we see if everything works right away user local s bin backup and we call it backup locks the exterior until we append each day in we could also add here some Unix timestamps for further purpose but you get the idea this is just to see if it works or not. So save the file. Let's see if we have here some errors in it. Before we can use such sh files we have to add here the change mode to warm because here when we list it it's not exactly doable. Therefore we have to change it to x as you can see here now it can be executed you can execute it with dot a slash and now backup this let's see if it works. It doesn't work Okay, let's see cut back up locks the exterior this file is created but the user local s bin node read no read data flows is not working because I've had to do something wrong once again backup.sh doesn't work as expected let me see why. Next mistake because your the folder can't be exists because I have missed here n slash Dan certs tryin yay, here we have it 22 backup chasen tomorrow. And then we will create here the backup dot JSON 23. So let's see if it also has the content what we want. Let me see if I can find you on this is on our node read I think then we change it to is the backup working? Finished? Then clear. Then once again the backup then cuts and is the backup working? Very good. And now we could go into nano and we say EDC Chrome tab. And now we could add here for example, that every day at 230 in the morning. The route should be executed the user local A spin backup backup got its age. Now I would like to test it if it works each minute or if we have some problems then we get rid of the documents and also from the backup locks then we're waiting a minute and there we go on the file is executed the last time line 35 And it's created 959 53 perfectly so our backup routine is working properly. And now we get in each day. Of course we have to edit your nana etc crontab Yeah, it's working. So for example, Ceridian and two in the night because often in the nighttime store is not so much traffic and we could back up here.

# SEPARATION OF TASKS OF SOFTWARE AND HARDWARE

So for all of the practical examples, I follow one rule, and that's called a separate tasks, I try to focus on the MC use original tasks. That means the MCU should only send me some data from some sensors, or will control and servo, motor, controller, motor, etc. And the rest of the logic will be made in Node rates. And of course, you can have your web server on it. You can also use WebSockets, you can use your telegram bot, you can make HTTP requests, all the stuff can be done on the ESP 32. But in my case, it's much more flexible and convenient to do it on the node read side, because you will see the main advantage later on in a practical example.

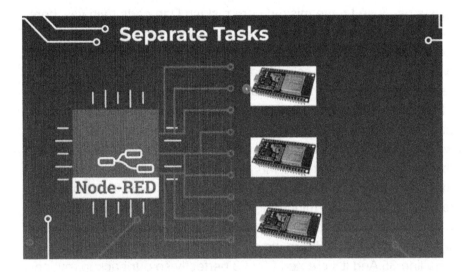

For example, in the minivator station, we're just sending data via encoded data node red, here, not red, I can make here some hysteresis, I can make some calculations. And then sending back for example, the ESP 32 listens on a callback from an encoded data topic if and fan or air conditioner should turn on or off. And the logic is here. So I have no trouble and hassle to change the logic and sent one or zero if the air condition should go on off. If I have everything on the MCU Of course, I can flesh it over the air, but then you have to be directly in the near of your microcontroller. And if you have really a lot of smart home things running on your home sites, then it's not easy to change every MCU at once. In node red, we change the logic and everything on the MCU is the same because we're just delivering turn on the acquisition on off and what happens here is directly in Node red and it's the same in the setting where we watering our plants.

# FIRST OVERVIEW OF FLOW AND NODES

I would like to show you what you can do and how the node read is set up. First of all, you have here the flows and the menu on the right there is some plus you can add your some flows and was describing you have here the menu what you can do with the flows, for example, you can see list all hidden flows, you can also say, I would like to show only that flow which is active active, then you could say all other flows are highlighted. And then you can see you're here, only the flow line is here, then you can say all flows should be shown. And then you see all the other flows, which we are done later on, we'll do in our node read. Yes, if you want to delete some flows, you can go to the hamburger menu right on the top. And then you can say, for example, flow, delete, you also can double click on it, and then you can delete it, double click on it, you can change the name, double click and delete it. And this is how you can edit the flows. But I would like to show you here how we can formulate your flows inside. And then we have on the left side and the menu. When it's not here, you can toggle it with the mouse in the middle of the palette, then you can show it. For example, what we are using here, can here for Filter Menu, then we type in inject and can drag and drop here, one of these nodes inside our dashboard, then right on the right button, you can hear increase the size so that it's more convenient to see. And then what we do, we can connect the flows. And what we have here we have an here an inject node, which triggers us our flow and here we have an DPAC node. And whenever we do something, you can see here some blue circles. That means that the flow is not deployed, how can we deploy it on the right top corner, we click on deploy. And then we have our flow. Here on the left side, on the menu, we have different kinds of icons. And I click here on this pack, debug messages, and then we click here on the left from the timestamp. And we injecting here the Unix timestamp in seconds, or milliseconds. When I click on the timestamp, you can see here, the server date. I click once again. And you can see three seconds later. Double click on timestamp. I can change here from timestamp to string. And could say for example, here string Hello World finish. Don't forget to deploy again. And then HelloWorld you could also add here some shortcuts with Control and Enter you can click on finish and then risk control and D you could deploy for example you also have here a small triangle you can change here, for example, the whole node red should be deployed only changed flows, or only changed notes. And this is what I normally select only changed nodes you can see it here on this left I can change the to change flow that means everything on this flow will be deployed, or or the whole node red will be deployed. And it's not necessary to deploy the whole node red because we are always working here mostly on one flow. What's also very handy when you for example, putting out here and switch and you don't know what does this switch nodes really do. Then you can click here on this control info I can and you see here some not some some texts, some documentation, what is all about? And it's really really handy. And although normally men are not using any documentations here it's really really handy because you want to know Aha, what's coming out what's coming in and how can I change here the settings etc. So also on the hamburger menu on the right here we have some input and export. This is also very cool because you can use your my finished flows, you can click on input. You could import the JSON or just copy and paste here. The chasen click on input and then you have the new flow insight. You know read the same with export you could export it the actual flow click on Download for example, or you can click on the file.

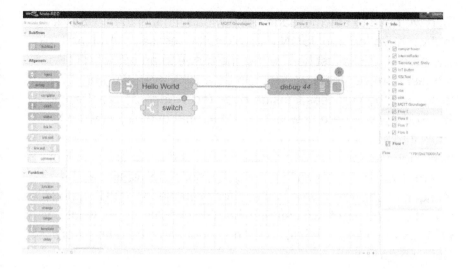

And now when I'm imported, as you can see, you could enter here the JSON and then you can change and also give someone else your, your flow. It's in the meaning of the open source. And also if you have some questions and want to share your flow then this will be the preferred way. Yeah, also we are using here is when we are installing some nodes will click on installation and searching the node for example, the telegram bot, and then we can install it and when it's installed, then we could search it on the left side. And then it's here also available. If you're importing something into the node is not installed, you can't deploy it. Then you have to before install it, then you can deploy it and then the flow will work correctly.

# PROCESS JSON

Let's cover Another example. And we have now the case that we get from an API and JSON. And this JSON should now be processed. Therefore, I'm not copying this function, I'm adding a new function. So for example, this will be called JSON. From API, which are simulating it, already have prepared some JSON. So just copy and paste it in. It's called node read, course, we could change it. Mosquito through mosquito diversion and the users pics lady, you can add here, whatever you want, it's just training purpose. And

41

then we have to say message dot payload, equals to my JSON, so that we have fee and JSON and return the message. And, as I told you before, this is just here is the line between an official HTTP request from weather data, Bitcoin data, whatever you want to fetch, and then process it inside node red. And therefore, I would like to show you here how we can do it. First of all, I just want to show it to you on the debug 50. So timestamp, will trigger the whole flow, then we see the node cause object, and there are nested three different variables. It's called mosquito mosquito version and mosquito user. Then we could use for example, an HTTP in no HDP in that was not right, we can use the also chasing, that's what I want to show you. Next, the buck 51. And connecting the output here, sir. Here we go.

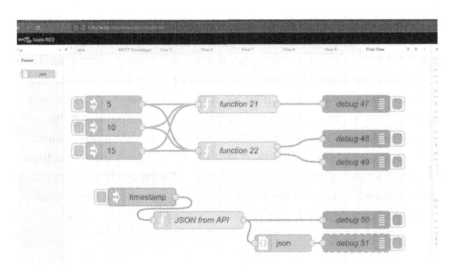

On deploy. And now we see the chasen will be now transferred into a string, if we want to send it for example back or we want to edit it later on. What we also can do now is I'm adding yet another function. I would like to access one of the data. So we are training here, getting you the data from an API. And now I want for example, access the user, how can I do that, double click on it. And then we could say here, let's use on is message that payload, and here we have the very first object is called node read course. And the nested object is called mosquito user. And this is how we could access here the value of pixel Edie semicolon and now I could say if user

42

equals to pixel ad and then we could say message dot payload is access granted else message dot payload is Access denied. And what we created here is just in simple logic, we get something from an API we are testing it if n state is true or not true or is the case the user so then we d activate those tools so that we only getting a debug 52 Let's see Access granted. And if we have here for example, in this chase and not pics lady pixel editor one, then access is denied. And now we can add to some logic, then we can send for example and Boolean false or true back to our ESP via M Quiddity. And can start here and the fan in air conditioner hours.

# CONTEXT, FLOW AND GLOBAL VARIABLES

In node red, we have different kinds of scopes. That means our variables in the function 23, for example, are only valid in the function 23. And I would like to show you the different kinds of scopes, what we have and how we can use it. So here, we have the scope. And we need in here an inject node and function node and as well as the back node. So the first scenario will be, we are sending here some temperature data. That's just number. And it's called temperature. And for example, we have here 25 degrees, these 25 degrees, I would like now to change in the function. And of course, this works because we are sending data from left to right. So let temperature one is the message dot payload. And we add in three, for example, just for training purpose, then we say, lead new message that we can also practice this one and say New message dot payload, of course, we could overwrite the existing one. But you could also see what we can do temperature one, and we're returning to New message.

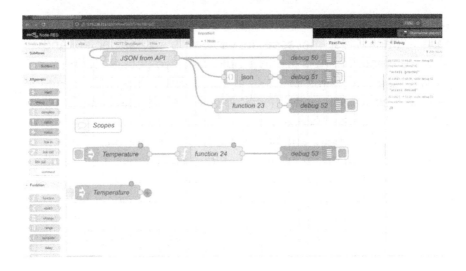

So when we are sending now the temperature, we're getting 28, because 25 and override it in this function, and we will get in yet Deepak 50s results. Okay, now, next scenario, this was the local scope, what if I would like now access the temperature one variable in the function 25. So when I would like to make here and node one, temperature one, you can see here, it's not can not find name temperature one. Why is that? So because we have declared here, but it's not in an adult, it's not in an flow scope. And I can deploy it here, I get here. An error indication, if I make this, I see a reference error or temperature, one is not defined. So what we can do now is, next one, I copy the temperature, and our new function notes, and also n debug nodes. Then we link those together, function 26. And now, we have here some context in the context. So that you'll see what I mean here is the context is local, the flow is in the flow, and global, or have no regrets. And now we say for example, they're not let we say variable, it's an wider scope. Office light is global dot get, and we sing office lights, this is how we access and global variable. And then we have to say if type of Office light is undefined, because when it's not created, we running into an error. And if this is the case, we say office light is zero. And then we have here and zero, and now we can work with it. And we could, for example, toggle it and with toggle I would like to create here and a random number, meth floor and I say meth random equals two so that they only get here and one or and zero out of it.

44

```
 3    gtobat = att ur noue-reu
 6
 7  */
 8
 9  var officelight = global.get("officelight");
10  if(typeof officelight == "undefined")
11      officelight=0;
12
13  let rnd = Math.floor(Math.random()*2);
14
15
16  return msg;
```

And now I say if round the random number equals to one then two global sets off his light is true. Else global sets of his lights you get it is false. So and then message payload is random. So what I have done here is I created here and random number and saved the number directly into and global variables as you can see here 110111 sub now to show you how we can work with that I am adding here and delay. And you will get the idea what I'm trying to show you here, then adding here and a new function and also an debug so that we have a better purpose. I changed here to delay from two seconds, because now we changed here their random number and assigned it to our global office light. And here I would like to access these global variable. Therefore, bar. Office light is global, and now I get Office light. And now I could say if it's not assigned then equals to zero. And if office light is available, because we send a true or false, then we could say message payload turned on else message payload is turned off and return the message. So if I'm now triggering these flow, I will get here and random number and this random number will be shown here in debug 54. Two seconds later, I'm accessing the global variable in the function 27, which is assigned in 26. And we'll print it out in debug 55. Let's see if it work. Message one is globally assigned and we have here turned off. So we have somewhere and a logical mistake. So let's check what we have done here. Haha, office lights I have to spell it right. Next Ryan sera turned off one and accessing turned on very good. And now we have access here on any global variable. And also if the function 27 is in an other flow, it will work nearly the same. But be aware we can store here data for our function in our smart home. But if the server unexpectedly or is rebooted and unexpectedly don't work anymore, because maybe the instance of Node red hung up or something like that, then also our variables in the global and context scope are vanished and be gone. Therefore, whenever it comes to critical incident, I recommend you to save the data in a flat file or in a database it's easier.

# SO MANY NODES

I'm not a fan of just theoretical, go through all of the notes and we'll introduce you to the different kinds of settings etc. By making it just theoretical, I'm more a fan of making practical examples and use different kinds of notes. And this is what we are doing now later on in the project. But one note, I would like to introduce you because it's really, really handy. And it's not the chasen, it's the, the join nodes. And I'm adding here for example, here and string number. Now, let's let's take one and two and also here we have three, and now, all of these three comes together to the join.

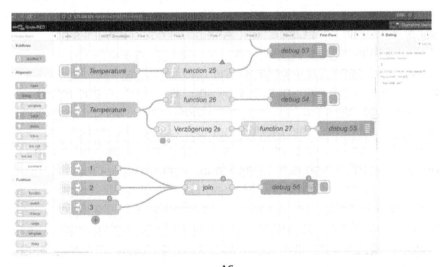

And what I would like to have here is I would like to collect each of them and if every one of these through inputs will be here, come to this join node and then I would like to have a message on the Deepak and this is what the join is doing here, then we are switching from the Modi to manual. And then we could say here different kind of things. For example, I would like to have three different values from each of the topics and then will be sent a copied message and this one will be not true because 123 message one no message two three next message, let's test it out. So one missing key here are what do we have here missed and key value. I've missed the topics here. So we have to add here the topic for example, this is temperature. Then here we have immunity and for example, AR quality. Then we click on deploy and then we click here on delete. Now temperature one will be assigned nothing happens air quality is delivered from another ESP nothing happens. And now with click on humanity, I get all of the three messages at one message in one object and this is exactly what we often need when it comes to different ESPs sending data I would like to collect the data and then save it once in the database. And of course when here the server will be shut down these three values will be lost. But to be honest, these are just sensor data's and we can live with that if one will be one data will be missed. So here we have a lot of different nodes. We will go through it in the practical examples.

# MQTT TERMINOLOGY

Let us start in this topic by defining a few terms about the MQTT and could the is called message careering telemetric transport. And M commodity is a lightweight messaging protocol that is designed to connect devices and sensors with low bandwidth, high latency or unreliable network connection. And it was on is used for machine to machine communication. And back later for a few years, we haven't got so much stability internet, our Wi Fi connection or network connection, and therefore the illiquidity has some security features in it was developed in 1999, by an IBM and also another company. And it's for monitoring and controlling remote devices, especially in the context of Internet of Things. And this is what we are also doing for our smart home. And it's perfected, designed for fast and reliable exchanging of messages. And M Quiddity is a publish subscribe messaging protocol. That means we need a broker, the broker handles the whole communication between the sender and the receiver. And one of the central things is also the topic because this is the target address, and the broker distributed to the topic to someone who published a message. So for example, in ESP 32, publish a message to the topic temperature, the broker handles the message and sends to everyone who has subscribed to this topic, the message. So that means it makes it ideal for use in situations where multiple devices needed to communicate with each other. But where bandwidth and network reliable D are not really here or limited. And this is also exactly what we have with this tiny ESP 32. Because we can't send too much payload and payload is also you defined is the content of the encoded message, coerces quality of service, we'll come to this later on. And we have the last one retained messages. And as the term already says, The broker holds back the message until an client goes online with some certain topic and then the broker publisher sends it to the subscription.

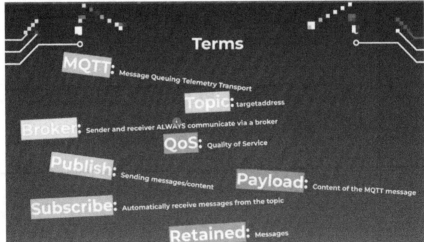

And this is what an retained message is. So all M coded D has become one of the I think most and widely used IoT protocols. Because of its simplicity. It's absolutely flexible. It's open source when we are using them. Mosquito server, for example, a mosquito broker, and it's also had some wide range of platform and programming languages. So can use and Quiddity with PHP, for example, with Python as well as also no GS implementation. So and of course, also his C++ in the Arduino environment. And this makes it really, really flexible for IoT devices. Later on. We go a little bit more in detail about every point.

# MQTT NETWORK USING THE EXAMPLE OF SUBSCRIBER AND PUBLISHER

Let's talk about the equity network a little bit more in detail. And we'll make right after this explanation and real life example. So first of all, we have here our mosquito broker, and it could be run on server on Raspberry Pi. And of course, it's also in on reserve or online. Nevertheless, it has to be reached from our clients. Then we have here our topic, for example, ground floor and temperature, then we have here and DHD, 20, temperatures and so on. And of course, this has to be attached on an MCU. And the MCU sense now in an interval, for example, each five seconds, the actual temperature, and this is called publish, and this publish will be done to this topic, and has the value 28. So the broker now gets in unregular, five seconds, the 28th, or the actual temperature. On the right side, for example, we have other devices, for example, a smartphone and other PC and tablet, and also maybe another device, because on this ESP 8266, for example, isn't really attached with an air conditioning, or an FEM, and this device subscribes now to the same topic and get instantly when the new temperature is here arrived, gets the new published temperature can process the value on maybe starts the air conditioner. On the above, for example, maybe we have here, some dashboards, etc.

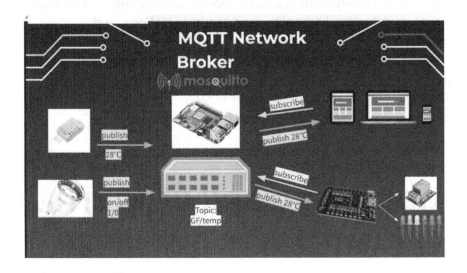

So one message will be published to the broker. And because these devices are subscribed to them commodity broker, they are getting automatically the values from the broker. And of course, you could also have yet another device as well, you could have hundreds of devices. And for example, this isn't smartplug does publish one on and off. And also those devices can subscribe to multiple topics. And therefore, we can have multiple topics. So this one is not publishing on temperature. This one is maybe publishing for ground floor and socket office, so that we know if the socket is on or not. And this is now the main introduction. And now we want to make here an example. I've already logged in into my server. And in this server I have fear and Docker container. So it depends on if you have mosquito installed on the regular basis, then you can get your mosquito pup for example. Or in my case, it's not found and I have to jump directly into the Docker container. And this could be done by a Docker exec it here, then the name of the Docker container and SSH because I want into the bash. Let me see if this right yeah, now I'm directly into the mosquito container. And now I can add here some basics commands, I've added here and an inject node and M Quiddity. Out and M Quiddity in with the same topic, and here I getting my first m Quiddity. So let's recall it Deepak first m Quiddity. And when I'm clicking now on the inject node, I'm sending here and original timestamp. I also consent the and string for example, hello from node red. Then I'm sending in a once again and via node red, I'm sending fraud to the mosquito broker. Here I getting the message back and sending into an epoch and you can see hello from not red. But the interaction we could also make here on the comment line. So for example, I could say mosquito pup for publish local host or the IP address from the server. In this case, I'm directly on the service I can use localhost. Then we say the topic, it's called first equity team. Then we have a message Hello, from a CLI. Then the user with a small you it's called pixel ADM. And then to be aware, not on small p and lower p and high p because this is the password the other parameter is the port. So So password. This is no dreads cruise. And when I'm sending now you can see here hello from CLI once again. So I also can interact here directly from the server to the browser. But it can also go in the other direction. Let's see here we have an add an inject node. And we want to send hello from C CLI into a second, M Quiddity. And you can see here I have no other debug nodes. And I would like to subscribe via command line. So mosquito sub in this case, localhost topic is the second input to then the user. Then we have the passwords. And of course, it could also put the other things in apprentice so that because there are also strings, so let me see if this everything is correct. Looks good so far. And when I'm clicking here, from hello from CLI, you can see two times once hello from CLI, then we could change it here for example, hello, volume to just one click. One click and it's directly here. Perfect. This was also a good example how we can use the M Quiddity.

# MQTT TOPIC LEVELS AND WILDCARD WITH CLI EXAMPLES

Now we're gonna talk about the M crudity topics. First of all levels are separated within slash. So for example, this is one string, and we can send it on ground floor office and temperature. And this gives us the ability later on that we can filter the messages. So what I mean with that we building here and the kind of hierarchy, that means, we have a ground floor, and then the ground floor we have different for example, rooms. And in the room, we have different kinds of sensors. That means, when we are building our smart home, it makes sense to have your such hierarchies because we can use your single wildcards what I mean with that, for debugging purpose, or also for our dashboard. It's really handy when we have here such an hierarchy. And as you can see, the blue ones are indicating the floor, then we have the yellow ones, the yellow one is the different kinds of rooms and the white ones are always giving us the temperature. And with the single level wildcards, you can use the N plus sign instead of the rooms. And we getting all of the messages. And this is really really cool debugging and also for dashboard purpose in and fields, we can here subscribe to this topic, and getting the office kitchen hallway and bathroom.

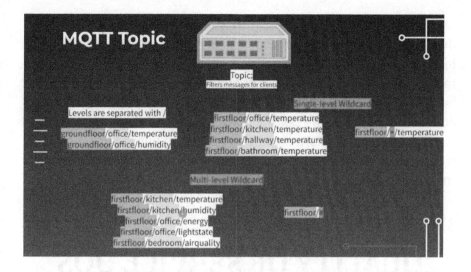

**MQTT Topic**

Topic: Filters messages for clients

Levels are separated with /

groundfloor/office/temperature
groundfloor/office/humidity

Single-level Wildcard

firstfloor/office/temperature
firstfloor/kitchen/temperature
firstfloor/hallway/temperature
firstfloor/bathroom/temperature

firstfloor/+/temperature

Multi-level Wildcard

firstfloor/kitchen/temperature
firstfloor/kitchen/humidity
firstfloor/office/energy
firstfloor/office/lightstate
firstfloor/bedroom/airquality

firstfloor/#

Also, we have here multileveled wealth wildcards. This is with the hashtag. And as you can see here, we have also the first floor, we have different rooms, but also different topics. That means temperature, humidity energy, here, we have always the same as temperature in the middle. But here we have the wild card at the end, that means everything what is published on the first floor, I will I would like to get. And the important notice is that this only works for subscriptions, not for publishing. So we can't publish to each of the things because we don't know if everything we want has subscribed. So therefore, it's only valid for a subscription. So enough the theory, let's test this in and real life example. I've created here in Node red an example with the first wildcards so that means that we have here and a single level wildcard with the plus as we did before, I have here, for example, first floor first first first floor with kitchen, office, hallway bathroom, and everyone has in temperature. Here I have the wildcard the first row wildcard and temperature. And here is the debug. That means when I'm clicking here on kitchen, we getting the kitchen, when I'm clicking on the office, this is Justin's doing bathroom, hallway, hallway, kitchen. And normally, we are getting here to temperature on this topic, but you get the clue out of it. The same thing will work and deleting here and then debug sin was to multi level wildcards. As you can see here, I have Office 123 and four. Here we have lights, temperature shutters, and the air quality. And single wildcard is the multi wildcard is on second floor so that I get in everything on the second floor on the output. So when I'm clicking here at getting the office light, the temperature, the shutters, and here, also the air quality. And this is really cool when it comes to an debugging purpose. Or as I told you before, for example, in a dashboard so that I only need one line of code to getting all of the current deliveries from the second floor. Really, really cool feature could be handy. And this is necessary when you're building up your own smart home that you keep in mind that filtering the topics can be useful.

# QUALITY OF SERVICE QOS

So the N Qt T provides three levels of quality of services to ques for message delivery, which allows publisher and to control the reliability and consistency of messages, and also what are delivered to the subscriber. And the three quest levers are quest zero, at most once quest one at least once and cool as to exactly once. So let's take a closer look on the first one quiz null. This is my preferred variants, and at most ones means that we are just sending from the client to the broker, one publish and we are not knowing if it's delivered on it. That means this quest level guarantees that the message is delivered at most once to the subscriber. The publisher sent messages with coo coo as zero by simply sending the message to the broker without waiting for any acknowledgement for the subscriber. That means we don't know if it's there or not, we just showed it. And the broker then forwarded the message to everyone who has subscribed. However, the broker does not keep any record of which subscriber received the message. And he does not retry sending the message if any subscriber fails it. So why I'm using this one, because the equity protocol license TCP and TCP already made and 300 handshake that means if I'm online, I know not really for sure, but I know that the connection is stable enough to send it because an coolest one take a closer look we have here also an acknowledgement of from the broker. That means the coolest level guarantees that the message what we are sending here is delivered, at least the ones by the subscriber publisher sends messages from the quest by sending the message to the broker and waiting for an acknowledgment with this pop back from the broker. The broker then forwards the message to all the subscribers who have subscribed. And then if the subscriber fails to receive the message, this is now what's the coolest level one is then the pop back is lost and the broker will resend the message until the subscriber acknowledged the message. And in this case, you could duplicate your messages because if this is Get lost the publish will be cloned a second time and then it goes out to become possible. And then of course, we have the last one took us through exactly once.

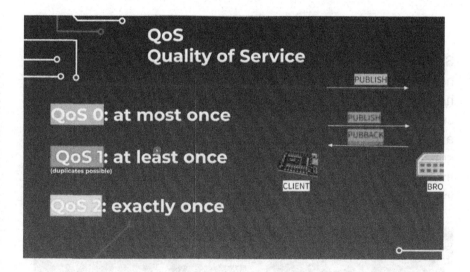

And as you can see here, we have here a two way handshake for example, the class level guarantees that the message is delivered exactly once to the subscriber. So the publisher sends a message request by sending the message to the broker. Here we go and waiting for the handshake involving the two step acknowledgments. So the puppet req will be received and then the client sends back a ha okay I release it. And if it released we got also here and publish completed and then everything is ready and over four sending it that means the broker will resend the message onto the circuit subscriber will until as a flow acknowledged the message was to pop comp, this level of QoS is the most reliable of course, because you have to hit that handshake. But also it costs us bandwidth and time and network traffic. So in summary, Cu S zero is the least reliable but the fastest one QoS is more reliable, but of course little bit slower until we have the most reliable but slowest and most resource intensive variant. And the choice of course depends always on what you were building. In my case when we are sending sensor data who has zero is absolutely okay because it doesn't matter. If one sensor data is be missed. In the next few seconds, I got an updated version so doesn't really matter. But if you really have some critical infrastructure points.

# RETAINED MESSAGES

So what are retained messages, retained messages as we can see here we have the same setup as before. With your broker, we have here some sensors, and we have here and clients, the publisher sends now the temperature value with an retain flag to the broker and the broker saves the value. And in this case, the client has not subscribed. So retain messages are really useful for an application that require request that the latest state, in our case to 32 degree of information is available to the subscriber.

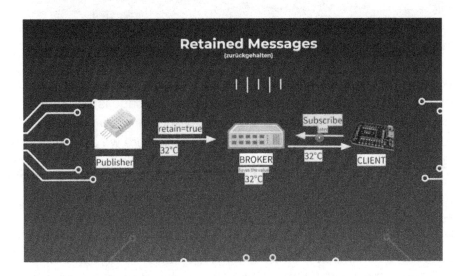

But even if the subscriber weren't subscribed at this moment where the messages are published, because normally when it's published, the broker immediately delivers to the clients the the project, but the subscription is at the moment when it's published, not really subscribed and therefore, when we have learned this device, and later on the client subscribe to that topic, it will immediately get the 32 from this value the last value is will be stored and this is an good point when you need fast responses for example, but also take in consideration that it can be confusing, because when you're not managed properly, for example, if a retained message is published with a value that never changes could be possible for example, some the doors open the window is closed etc and this will be not changed for a few hours. Then it can be misleaded by new subscriber who may assume that the message is deleted state of the system. So therefore, retain messages in my case should only be used when it makes sense for the specific use cases and the topic should be chosen carefully. And I show you later on in the practical examples where you can fetch with the client actual new data so that you don't really use the retained flecked but so in summary, retained flex may could be handy in some cases.

# BIRTH DEATH UND LAST WILL

Let's talk about the birth death and last will messages. So, in general when we are going to the server we have here some messages and we could change for example the birth death and last will messages so the birth feature means that the allows a client to specify a message. So when we establish the connection and this message is called The Birth methods the birth method can be used to indicate that the client has connected successfully or to provide information about clients can be deleted so, for example, we could here say connection I'm online let's see what happens if I'm making here talk I'm online because now I started as you can see, we using these messages not for the clients for the whole program. Just to see that you can see here the example interesting in my case I think is also I'm deleting this this is the last will of course we have also a death the death is when we are disconnecting it on intentionally but what's really interesting is what happens when the connection is unintentionally lost disconnected unexpectedly, this method is called the Lost will message this last will message is sent by the broker to any subscriber of the topic indicating that the client has disconnected X unexpectedly so MQ D for been known is broken for example so when we are now for example, here is our patina now unexpectedly kill or stop the mosquito server. Then as you can see here MQ today is broken and I got connection if we started all over again here we go. Nothing is right away. Let's I'm online Tech, we are back. Once again mosquito we kill it and we getting you know includes this broken, why not? Let's start it all over again. Then we should get here I'm online.

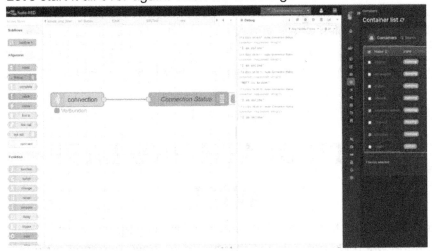

And our key because the process is absolutely killed but we stop it from as okay, because the broker is sending the message if something happens, and when I'm killing it, it has no chance to check the last wills. So you see, it's not really reliable, but in the case, you want to have fear and last will and then client disconnected unexpectedly. Then you can have here in one topic here and message so it gives you an good debugging purpose and also in your dashboard. You can see if a client has here, unintentionally or unexpectedly disconnected from your program.

# MQTT BEST PRACTICES

Let's talk about best practices in M quality. And the first thing is, don't use any slashes at the beginning because this means an empty level. So it doesn't make any sense to get rid of the first slash. The second one is, don't really use here, some spaces, and it will work, of course, but you always have to think, maybe on a system on a command line, how will be interpreted this space, it makes you headache, always in programming, don't do not use any spaces. So the best debugging and problem solving is to not making any problems in architecture. And therefore it's also not recommended here to use your son, for example, underlines or for example, you can say, first floor, kitchen, etc. This is not how you should set up your equity architecture. It's better to use your slashes as we seen before, so that you can have here some filtering mechanism and always make clear names for example temperature, or for example, it's the room sensor, so that you know, aha wants to get here I get here multiple sense values within JSON.

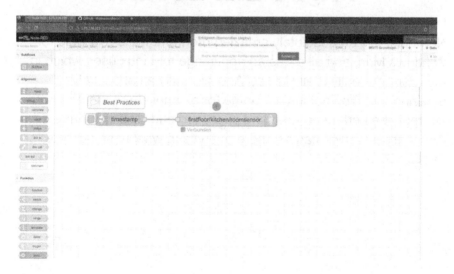

And this is better also be aware of any special chars. So it depends on which language is you're, you're using and of course, it is a special char will work on different kinds of system, but as we talked about the spaces be aware, if for example, in my case, the UTF act is used also on the server backends How can I address it with the command line for example, when there is often the back end server side is in English, the language is the native languages in English and therefore, often it's not easy to address it in this way. Also be aware to not overcomplicate the infrastructure for example, kitchen, left side top and then we have air quality or something like that, because then you have to work a lot with wildcards and this is also not what it makes very uncomplicated short names do not use for example first floor, room, kitchen, left and then send so it should be a really and precise name for example only kitchen, kitchen one that etc. Or the Office, Office and the number 23 et cetera. Oops. And this is it. As always in the it keep it clear. Do not overcomplicate it, and then you have also later on and good overview because often when it comes to IoT and smart home, it will grow very, very fast and you're not getting a good overview and then it will be an hustle to fix all the issues.

# MQTT EXPLORER

I would like to introduce you to the M quality Explorer from Tomas Nordquist. It's an absolutely amazing program. It's is available for Windows Mac, and also has an app image for Linux user, which in my case, it's really really handy. And it's really an absolutely amazing tool. You put in your name for example here the IP address the port, username and password and click on Connect. And that's it you we can see here everything what is on our topic so far.

And you see here I have fear and Shelley connected and this is interesting, because I see here uh huh, I have let me see for these three topics 101 messages, here we can see what is published, which clients are connected or how many subscription retained messages etc. And then let us send you something. So for example, let's see some a little bit out for example, here in our kitchen, when we are sending you some stuff, then we see also here, first floor, one topic, kitchen temperature, office, hallway always, and so on and so on. And convenient thing about equity to explore is that we can observe everything what is going on and our equity broker. It's especially handy when it comes to the smart blocks, Raspberry Pi's, etc, when we are not really sure what is going on on our whole equity broker. Therefore, we can inspect it here. And we can see what is going on. And what is the message and also for debugging purpose you can see here, which version, how long it's on, et cetera, really, really handy and absolutely amazing tool. And also with the license you can use it when I'm writing for. I think it's open source and also for let me see what is the license also for commercial purpose, I think. Yeah, launderettes. Absolutely perfect. Take a closer look will be handy for every am Quiddity project

# BROKER SETTINGS AND MQTT IN & MQTT OUT

Let us now make the configuration for the M Quiddity program. Therefore, we are putting in M qotd in and an M Quiddity out. And I would like to have the two R one inject node and one in debug Node, then we assuming in a little bit so that we can see here something. And there we go. So, first of all we want to configure the M coded a program, as you can see here we have here and red triangle, that means there is no configuration, double click on the node. And here we can choose on server, IP or different kinds of servers, you can click on New and commodity broker, I will edit the existing one, you will get here to the overview of the settings. And first of all we are entering here and IP address from your server. If you're using Raspberry Pi on local machine, then you can add here, of course, also local host. The port is usually 1883 Depends on your Docker installation or on your configuration on the system. The protocol in this case is 3.1 point went.

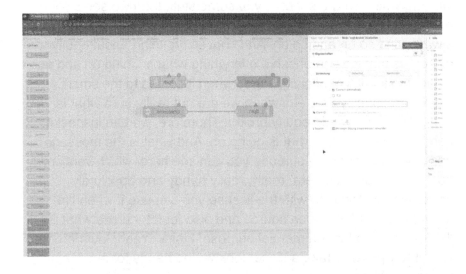

And I'm not using TLS. This is in separate an extra project at the very end of this online course. And the this are the settings for this step. We're switching to security and we're talking writing here our username and our password because we have the Emperor the mosquito broker with an authentification. If you haven't got any out edification, that's not what I recommend, but when you have, then you can leave this blank. Here we come later on. That's just for the first beginning, we click on refresh, and then we can add and select the the encoded a program then we could say for example, Hello World and click on finished. If you have entered here and encoded a program, it will be available in all other and quality notes as well. Then we can go and deploy. And as you can see, here it is I'm connected and the M Coti team. Note this is exactly what we want. So if we have some troubles for example, with the security then you can see there is no connection possible. So take a closer look on the authentification and also which IP address you are using. Finish. And we click on deployment and we have the right configuration for the M Quiddity broker

# SAVE DATA FROM NODE-RED IN INFLUXDB

In this project we want to save some values into influx dB m therefore, we have to install the influx DB node we go to installation and search for influx dB m in fee Lux there we go in flux DB node red contribution, click on install and then on the left side we can search it InfluxDB InfluxDB out then we want to have an inject node we want to have Elsa and function nodes and also some M qu TT is because we are simulating yes something there we go. So, what we are doing now is I have here and timestamp and function and an equity out and we are simulating that we get some random numbers from an ESP, but here we have simulating in western static project. So afterwards, we can't just take our ESP 32 Send it to an M quality level and we haven't finished example. So therefore, for example, we setting here temperature the rights and quantity broker Cu S zero return false finished, and also here we are getting in temperature. So we are sending from node red directly to temperature, some values and getting it directly back. This is just for training purpose. So these two books were well. Now here in the functional, I would like to have here, some random numbers. So that we have a little bit better an example. Let random equals So for example, we take 30 to minus 20 plus one multiplies math random and at the end being 20.

And with this formula, we get values from 20 to 35 in a random manner, then we say for example, message payload is random. And then we are taking a closer look if this is already working with node one. With node one, we are getting the output directly here into the debug nodes. We're getting in an error from the influx DB node this is okay. So let me test it here. 2723 30 looks good so far. We can add here and pass integer. So that we have here no floating well use. Let's test it again. Yes, and here we have our random numbers. Okay. So for the simulation, we are finished, these values will be sent via encoded data from temperature to temperature. And now we are focusing on the influx DB connection, double click on it. And here we have different influx DB values, you can click on new influx dB. And here we go. We're taking in here the 2.0 the host is the IP address for my server. And see we have not the localhost with the port 8086. I'm not verifying my server certificate, because I have no SSL here. And then we are open with 8086 Our InfluxDB instance. It's called admin. It's not called admin picks lady Yes. Then we want to have fun token on the left side, you can choose your API tokens. Then we are clicking Generate token custom API token. And we have one packet installed.

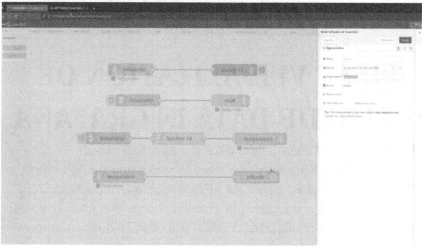

So in this packet, I would like to have read and write access, we'll click on Generate and then we are copy here their token. This token is only visible once so this button doesn't really work for me. That's the reason why I marked it highlighted in copied. Let's see fits in the clipboard? Yes. returns you right back to node red, and can fill in here the token. That's it. That's all what we want the bucket or the organization. Let me see what is the organization. It's under about? It's pixel at em. It's no dread is the bucket, you can also take a look here on buckets. And you also can create new buckets. It's like the data base system or the table. And the measurement This is that what we are later on using in an audit, so for example, here, I taking temperature, while us, we click on finish, then we click on deploy. Let's see if everything works. So we putting in here, a few values, I would say we'll double click on it, then we can go here on repetition, and I take an interval of five seconds that we get here, a few random numbers inside. Let's see if it if this works. Yes, it works. Then we're switching back to our influx dB. We're clicking here on data source. Then on the bucket, node red, we're filtering here, filtering here, temperature values. This is exactly what we are just created with you and William. Then we click on Submit. And there we go. I change the timeframe from one minute. And every five minutes or seconds, I click here and submit and I'm getting here a new value from 20. To 32 was the last value certitudes, the last value. So the 131 and as you can see, we're getting here our random numbers in InfluxDB.

# FIRST VISUALIZATION OF INFLUXDB DATA IN GRAFANA

Next step is that we use Grafana for visualization of our temperature data. Therefore, we have to make an new API token, we click on API tokens, generate API token, custom buckets, in the node red bucket, once again, generate and copy this one. Then we are choosing here configuration. And we'll click on data sources. And we click Add Data Source info flux dB, and here we are changing to flux. We are calling this samples this one, then I'm going a little bit down because I have in the clipboard to token, here's the token. So now, we can add here, the value for the world HTTP, double point and the port number. Then we are turning off the basic authentification. Because we have used the token and the organization is pixelated, the default bucket is called node red. And then we can make your first test, let's see, Data Source updated data source is working in one bucket is found safe and test. Very good. Now, we are getting here, our values in five seconds.

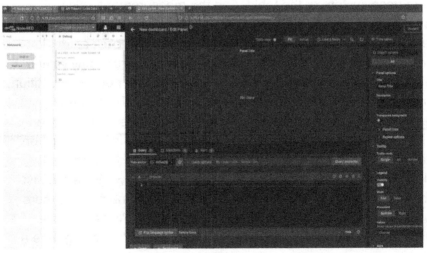

So therefore, I would like to add here and dashboards, we click on new new dashboards admin panel. And now in the influx dB, we click here on data source. And as we did before, are we searching here to node read the temperature value on the William, click on Submit. And as we can see, here, we are getting the data. And I click on script editor. And now we are getting near the influx DB material. That's what I want. Because here, I can add also the influx DB query. And this is all what I need. I click here on query inspector. looks very good. And there we go. We have here our values. Click on five minutes. The last one was 25. Let's see if this correct. So the 232. So now we can add some informations for example, that's the temperature. Then going a little bit down, I would like to have the Fill Opacity. Gradient modes can also mix. This one looks good point size that will be bigger. The units in my case it's Celsius that it actually can apply. Now I have here very easy to use. Graph. I can change yours for example to one minute. I think this is possible. I hear from now to one minute, but it's okay five minutes. But I want to do now is here refresh to close five seconds, so it will be automatically updated every five seconds. So let's see the last one was 20 seconds. What do we get now? 21. There we go. You can also add the and cycle view mode so that no menu is here. And you can share this kiosk view and therefore it's without a login also possible to visualize here and there was really cool and classic overview of your data.

# INSERT AND SELECT WITH MARIADB

In this project, now we want to store the temperature values, not in influx dB. But now in an MySQL, or Maria DB database. Therefore, we are installing the my SQL note. And this MySQL node is also working with Maria dB. Here we go. And now we have on the left side, that's my SQL. Here we have the notes, double click on it, then we are using your new one new MySQL database, for example, we could add em, then we have to add here the host, therefore, I take the IPM, the standard pod user is in my case root. And then we have to add the database, we haven't got any database, so we open at minor, or we can use it directly on the command line. In this case, the server is MDB. And we order the IP address. This is the Docker name. Then we click on login, we click on new database. And we could see here, temperature, we click on Save. And here we have our data base. And we can add here for example, on new table. And we could say for example, the name is ground floor office or what else we have here an idea with an auto increment, that means that each entry will get an unique number, this will be automatically incremented.

Then for example, we have an timestamp. And I would like to add the timestamp from no read and not directly from the database. And the last one will be the temperature. And I would like to have here we can use your floats as well. Okay, then we'll click on Save. And here we go. We have a our new data base with the table. So the database was ground floor, ground floor edit that was ground floor, then I click here on this one on no database, okay? Of course it's not, it's not ground floor, it's called temperature. And it's connected this is what I wants to see. So no dread has an valid connection to it, then we need here n function node because we can't directly access or install here data. Therefore, I'm just skipping that and

Deepak this is what I want. And in this file, we want to add here now the SQL statement. So an SQL statement will be stored in the topic. And when you're not familiar with the SQL statements just take a closer look in how this SQL statement will generate it we want to now insert into and now the table name in ground floor. Now we have to add here the values for example timestamp and temperature not the values the name of the fields. Now, the values I will add here. And then we could say for example here the value temp it's not created, but I will create it and this is the timestamp system for example and there we go have the temperature okay, so far, so good. Then we have to create those two variables. Then we say let temperature is message point payload because this is what we are generating with the inject node. And then we making your end timestamp timestamp. And the timestamp is made with meth floor so that we have a rounded number. And we're making a new date divided from 1000s because JavaScript gives us the Unix timestamp. I'm in milliseconds, but I wanted in seconds. Of course, we have to adhere get time. Okay, this is all what we need. So we're setting in here are our values. And afterwards we are getting the insert statements. Let's click here on finished. We clicking here on the debug. I don't want to I want to see it. No, I don't want to see it. Then. Let's see what happens. That looks good. We're getting here. This one and this one. Sounds very, very good. The node one here, we could get rid of it because we don't need it anymore. Once again, delete it. What do we get here? Two Unix timestamps Perfect. Okay. Then, what I would like to do now is to it's to the temperature. And afterwards, I would like to get the s, I, D back. So let's see what happens now. Object Object.

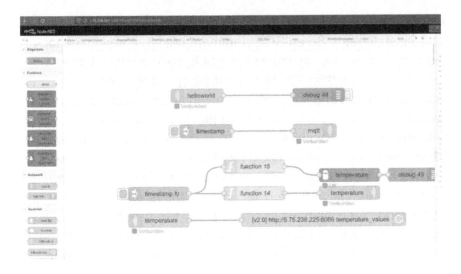

Okay, let's see if we have here. Some information here in temperature, ground floor. data's there we go on, but not right, we have here timestamp and temperature. Let's see, what do we have I missed here. Ah, that's the point. That's the point. Not directly here, I would like to have fit from Dr. Because he is our generator. Once again. Then click here on data. Here we go. So we deleting the false values because I don't need it anymore. And there we go. We get our fresh data temperature 25 chord this one is not useful. So now let's see what is the last value? Give me some fresh temperature values. No values. No Well, yes sir but now 12345 and 21. The last value is 21. There we go. And here we have our Unix timestamp, Unix timestamp, let's convert it. And there we don't Thursday, March 16. at GMT level, we have fifth year 15th and 18th. Perfect. That's what I want. And now we already have made an INSERT statement into from node red. And in the same manner, we could also use your own SELECT statement to get here values out from it. So let's take a closer look on this one as well. I make a next my Esquel then I would like to have you and Deepak then function and inject. Then tic tac we are linking each together. The MySQL is now the temperature then the function is message topic. Select from ground floor from temperature. Not ground floor, ground floor. And we say order. Order by ID DSC so that we get the last values at first, then we click here on Okay. Let's see if this works. But uh boom, and here we have an object where we get all 32 values with the ID, timestamp and the value again 25 is the last one. Let's check it once again. The last value is now 2530 that I haven't on Again at 29. And now we have here 30 was the last one. Exactly. And this could be also with an other function node behind the temperature. So between the MySQL and the debug Node, we could then access for example, the last values and also the nested objects. And this is how we use the node read with the MySQL or Maria DB

# RECOMMENDATION VS CODE WITH PLATFORMIO

Before we start right into the programming part, I would like to introduce you to Visual Studio code instead of using the Arduino IDE. And there is nothing bad of using the Arduino IDE, especially the two point version is looks nearly the same as the Visual Studio code, as you can see, but it isn't so fast. And I think also the whole programming experience is in Visual Studio code a lot better. So if you're using the Arduino IDE, and everything is fine, you can work with me along and also can use all of their libraries as well. When you're completely new to Visual Studio code, then I would recommend you to watch a few YouTube videos, because it takes a bit of time to set up all the necessary things. First of all, you need the extension platform I O. Because platform, you will take the whole communication part from the USB to our PC. And Visual Studio code is also on Mac OS and also on the most Linux distributions available.

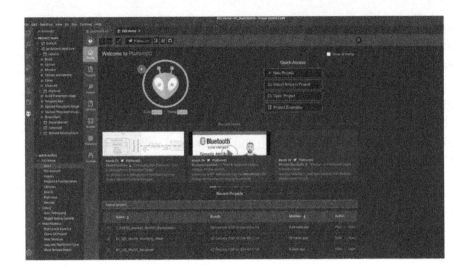

And when you're not liking the Visual Studio Code, there is also an of course, Visual Studio code is open source. But there's also vs codium. It's not from Microsoft. So you also can use this one when you're completely against Microsoft, but I totally can understand. But I'm using you the official Visual Studio code on a Linux distribution and install to the platform yo. And as you can see, we have also had the platforms we have the boats, the libraries, as well, as you might know it from your Arduino IDE. The good thing about this, that the whole programming parts, the whole thing was the IntelliSense etc, is much more faster. And not only that, also the compiler is really many, many times faster, then in the Arduino IDE. And this brings me also done point that the compiler in the platform your Visual Studio code, the C++ compiler is a little bit more stricter. Then, for example, in the Arduino IDE, so the Arduino IDE, for example, you could make here and function. And you could invoke this function before it's referenced. And here you are, for example you need and prototype etc. So I would say that the compiler year is a little bit more stricter a little bit more, you have to think about what you do with the prototypes, etc. But this is no handicap at all. And also when you want to use my codes in the Arduino IDE, There is one central main file it's called the platform your ini data and here we describe everything from our used MCU the monitor speed, the upload port, etcetera.

And also here will be referenced which libraries we're using. So you can take a closer look in the platform any you can open it with a text editor, nevertheless, what operating system you're using, and then you can see what libraries I'm referencing here in the in this project and then you can go into your Arduino IDE and can find the libraries as as he mentioned with the name or Vista name from the outer yeah here we have the CPP This is the main file and there is no ino file. And then we could start and all and everything will be done wire the blood from your desk menu on there you can create the new the the new project etc. So, take a few moments set up your platform or environment. It's really a time saver and you will enjoy the programming part a lot more instead of the other NVDI.

# LED BLINK WITHOUT DELAY

Let's start with our basic sketch, I have already created a new project, an empty project. And for this example, I'm using year, an

ESP 32. And D one is a small model, you can use every ESP 32, what you have, and I attached here directly and led to it. And of course, normally you meet here, and resistor. So that led doesn't get damaged. But this is my test led, and therefore, I connected it to the pin 26. And also to ground because now we want to test our code. So what I have already done is I have the platform in edit it for an AC delivery model, I've created the monitor speed, this is the port when you're here on Windows 10. You can see the port in the platform, you're on the devices when you're connected, like connect me or the ESP. We can see it now it's connected.

And when I click on refresh, now if you're on USB zero def Tatay wine, and you will when you're on Windows, then you get T and comport and then you can enter here for example, your comm certain for example. Then I have already insert the switch back and Library's analog right pops up client for the illiquidity later on, and are the new JSON, these are the standard libraries, which we're using in the projects, then, let's start with simple running pots, we would like now, making the LED flash in, for example, each two seconds or one second. Therefore, we are creating an global variable by the LEDs and pin 26. We starting to see where to begin. And then we have to set up here the Pin node. It's led and its outputs. Then, because we are using it the logic blink without delay, I would say we making you an unsigned, long previous Milly's. And we define it with the current runtime and you're jumping into the loop and now we are getting here the same unsigned long, but here the current in this and we are seeing is Millis then we're seeing if the current meal is minus the previous meal is no previous Millis is greater than for example, one seconds, then something should happened, what should happened first of all, we have to reset the previous release to the current release. So, that function will work again.

```
20  unsigned long previousMillis = millis();
21
22  void setup()
23  {
24      Serial.begin(115200);
25      pinMode(led, OUTPUT);
26  }
27
28  void loop()
29  {
30
31      unsigned long currentMillis = millis();
32      if(currentMillis - previousMillis >= 1000){
33          previousMillis = currentMillis;
34          digitalWrite(led, !digitalRead(led));
35      }
36
37  }
```

And then we are seeing here for example, digital rights then we think led and then we could say here for example, digital read entity. So, what have we done so far? Let me see if the compiler has any problems or are we right and when we have already uploaded our code, then we can see that the LED is flashing. So what have we done now, we have in the code set that the current release is the runtime in milliseconds minus the previous Milly's should be greater than 1000. So, that means, when the current run time is greater minus the previous minutes, which we defined here is greater than a second, then the if statement is true, and the LED will be turned on. How is that possible? Because we are setting here the output and then we are saying here read what current state do we have led if it is on then inverted If it is off also inverted it and so we can make with one line, that will be toggling. Then the previous minutes will be returned or reset so that in the next second, nothing will happen after this will be greater than 1000. And this is a basic logic where we can make a blink without delay.

# SEND AND RECEIVE JSON

One thing is for sure, when you are working with the ESP 32 Then we will also using JSON data. JSON is unstructured form where we can nest more data in unstructured way. Like here, we have here and key well, your first name and here is the content, John, first name Anna and so on and so on. And this is one single string, what we can use for transmitting data in unstructured form because later on, we can access these keys in an easy way. And JSON we can send it from not read but also from the ESP and I would like to show you both ways, because we will use it later on in our first example, and therefore, we simulating here now the data and later on, in the next example, we are using it right away. So therefore I'm doing here. One inject node one equity out one equity in and one debug note. So what I would like to do now is, I would like to send an chastened data from no dreads to the ESPN, so we call it Jason from node red. And I would like to receive it, this is the ESP values.

And we are sending here, not the data we are sending here and JSON file. And I've already prepared an simple JSON file, we click here on the three dots, you already can include it here, but with the three dots, we getting an visual editor. And here we have a four variables inside and chasen. It's called The first one is called device. And here is the ESP 32 is the best MCU. And this is a string. And here we have three integer values. And this is really the best example for our next project. I click on Finish, finish deploy. And now we already consented. But, of course, we have implemented yet in the ESP 32. And this is what I would like to do. Now I would like to implement that we can process the JSON in the ESP 32. Therefore, we have to subscribe to the JSON from node read topic. Let's see if we have done it. Up go. Subscribe, Jason from not read. Then, let's see where we are. Here we go. We should catch here the topic. If the topic is JSON from node read then you should have thumb sing. And now we are making our lives very easy. Because we are using the Arduino chasen website. And here's some perfectly assistance what we are using now. Click on assistant we are selecting an ESP 32. And the first thing what we want, we want to deserialize because we get the string and we want to deserialize we click Next chasen. And now I'm implementing and implementing here, the JSON structure with some sample data what I think it will be received. And then I click on Next you will get an overview. But this is what I want. Here we get the perfect output for our ESP 32, which we can copy. Going back to our code, paste it.

```
70
71    if (String(topic) == "JSONfromNodeRED")
72    {
73        StaticJsonDocument<128> doc;
74        DeserializationError error = deserializeJson(doc, input);
75
76        if (error)
77        {
78            Serial.print("deserializeJson() failed: ");
79            Serial.println(error.c_str());
80            return;
81        }
82
83        const char *device = doc["device"];       // "ESP32 is the best MCU"
84        int temperature = doc["temperature"];      // 33
85        int humidity = doc["humidity"];            // 98
86        int lux = doc["lux"];                      // 643
87    }
88 }
```

And this is all what we need. So what have we done now, we have here and static JSON document with the proper size 128 bytes, we are DC realizing and not input. In our case, it's the message temp. If there is an error, of course we get the error. And here we are already created some strings. And with the strings we can work on and can fetch it for example later on. If you don't want a year and char you also could make your own string later on. And what I have prepared here, I've made one string out of all of it. So it's called string output. It makes a string out of device cast a string to temperature to humidity and to looks and then we're making an zero print line. Output semicolon and that's it. That's everything what we have to do when we want to process and JSON data. So let's see if it works, upload the code. Then here we go, ceremony to open, connected to M Quiddity, perfectly switching back to our node red. And now when I'm clicking of inject, you see here, ESP is the best MCU search strategy suite, 9064 suite. And when I'm now changing, for example, to humanity is 14. And then we have access here of the community as a single individual variable, or here is the string concatenated. Very good. This is the first example. And also in the other way around. When we are sending here values to the no rat, it's nearly the same, we're clicking on main cpp and going to the loop.

78

And we are not sending here. The Publish, we're making here an helper function, it's called a sent M couldn t, well use so that we have a good overview of our of our codes. So send em quality values, then we go into the top, wide sent encoded data values. And now once again, we consulting the website out in a JSON. We go to the assistance, and now we're saying serialize stream the structure is the same. Next, next, and there we go, I have not to think about the size etc, everything will be done for me. And this will be insert here. And now one step before we say you know, char buffer, with 265, then we have fear and buffer element. And now we can send this serialized JSON to our node read with clients dot Publish. And now with the topic is ESP values, and the content is now the buffer element. So what we are doing here with the serialized JSON JSON is that we using the the content from the duck doc doc variable and put it into the into the buffer element. So it's called buff also uploads the content once again called is uploading and then included the connection should be made. And each five second we should be getting the values here we go. In unstructured form, as you can see him ESP 32 is the best. Very, very nice. What you can do now here is for example we could use here not fixed, we could say for example, random minus 2014. And also here, humility and from example 10 to 19 Nine. And with the locks, we could say for example, you will meet 20 and 850 as a maximum upload once again. And now we should see a different kind of values coming to our node right. And this is the perfect simulation for our next project. It's very good. So we have covered here, sending ESP values as JSON values to the ESP and from node red and also from ESP to not read in the other direction.

# TRANSFER SOURCE CODE FROM VS CODE FOR ARDUINO IDE

In this project, I would like to show you how you can use the code from the Visual Studio code and platform you in the Arduino IDE. And therefore I flashed now the ESP 32 with a blank sketch so that nothing is on it. As you can see here, no data will be transmitted. Now I'm jumping into the folder where my sketch is from the Visual Studio code. And as you can see, this is the structure. And the structure is always the same. Here's the blood from any you can open it with a normal text editor, nevertheless, what kind of operating system you're using. And here you can see a lot of information regarding the libraries, etc. Then as the next point, there's a source folder and this source folder is interesting because we can copy all of the data inside the source. And we can jump to our Arduino IDE folder, I just saved and blank example here. And these are some internal data's I don't know what these are used for. But what we see here is the inner data. So I paste here in the credentials dot age, the Wi Fi and quality and the main cpp.

```
39    Serial.begi
40    pinMode(led,
41    connectAP();
42    client.setServer(mqtt_server, 1883);
43    client.setCallback(callback);
```

And now what we are doing is the name of the inner data has to be the same as the folder and there is nothing in into the main you know, and we are renaming the main cpp into Arduino IDE dot Ino. What we can do now we can open it. And here I have the older version of the Arduino IDE. That's not what I wanted. But as you can see here, the credentials will be already loaded. What we are doing now is we are loading it in the Arduino IDE 2.0 with data open. And as you can see here, it's perfectly loaded also with our encoded data H credentials. And here's the inner data. And now it's already connected. I've tried to compile it, then we're uploading it. Let's see if this works without any errors. If there are some errors, then maybe it's because we have years some missing prototypes. And in this version, that it is also very fast. So let's see if the trends mitad data will be started because this is the last sketch and as you can see, it works very fine. Do we see here something in the serial monitor? When I'm going to inject? Yes, here we go on. We also see in here the data from the serial monitor. But effectively, this is all what you need to do. Of course you have to select here your proper port and the port of it. And that's all what you need when you want to change from Visual Studio code to the Arduino IDE

# MINI WEATHER STATION WIRING

First of all, let's take a closer look on the wiring. Here I have an ESP 31 d h one module, your the two modules. One is the lightning measurement for the BH 175 Serum and the BMP 180. This is an older version. And of course, you can replace it within 280. You just have to replace also the libraries later on in the source code, but it's nearly the same in the source code. Both of the modules are using E squared C. And as you can see, I'm connecting here the E squared C together, because each of the modules have his own e squared C address. So we can use the normal e squared C pins that means for the data line, we are connecting here both modules. And then we are connecting with the GPIO 21 on the ESP 32 boards on the pin 22 GPIO port 22. I'm connecting here the clock from the east quad cm pin.

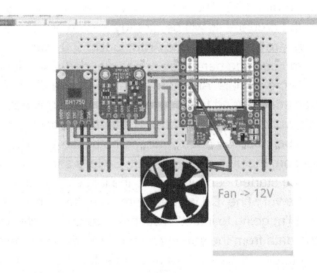

Fan -> 12V

And as you can see also here we are using a parallel for both modules, both of the modules will get to the ground and VCC and Vcc will get you from A false DC from the module and ground as well. Because we are powering our module within USB port, here fan computer and PC fan. And normally, it should be used here on

12 volt. But I can also connect it here on GPIO pin 18. So it only gets three points reward, but it's just for training purpose. And as you can see that there is something happening later on you can use in relay and then you can use of course, an air conditioner on ventilator. So let's take a closer look here on the Veyron. Here I have the sense on the PMP 180 and the light sensor and TAs the module on one line is missing. And that's all what we need for now. Here's the connection to the VCC and the ground and that's all what we need so far because later on, we're connecting the fence to it, but this will come later on

# BASIC SKETCH

I have here the basic sketch, the basic sketch has already implemented the Wi Fi and M Quiddity connection you can see here and, and file which called Wi Fi, M Quiddity dot h, it's an header data. And this header data, we paste here everything in what is recording the connection. So we need here, some includes, here are the statements for the encoded t part what we are needing, that's the server, our user and our password, and also the credentials dot h. And this we have included our Wi Fi for local access point the data the user and the password, then Wi Fi and reconnect function.

And these reconnect function will be used for the encoder team. And we use them later on here when we are subscribing to some topics, then this is the callback when you're sending from node red to our ESP 32 Some topics and some content that we can fetch here the topic name, here we have the connection of our Wi Fi and SSID and Password our the variables which we are defined in the credentials dot h in our main cpp now we are including the Wi Fi and Quiddity and then our unit JSON because we are needing later on and JSON as well. Then we are connecting the access point the equity part and in the loop we are just catch your if the equity broker is connected if not then we make an reconnect and incline connect in this part we have to blink without delay logic because often we are using here some logic very doing something according to the time and we are not using some delays some blocking delays in the loop therefore we are using here this blink without delay logic and here we are only having unsee reprint because later on when making you the encoded a publishing or something else.

# BMP180 TEMPERATURE AND BAROMETRIC PRESSURE

First of all, we start with the platform any year we have to enter analog, right, this is a standard in my platform in here because often we are using it later on, and therefore, it's referenced Pub Sub client for encoded data and powered, and we have the Arduino JSON. Then we need in here, the BM 085 library. And of course, when you're using the the BM 280, you have to find your according to your module, the right library. Then we are switching back to the main cpp and we're making a reference and we have to include the the wire dot h SPI H and Adafruit P mp dot h. And this will be referenced also from the example from this module, I'm sure you'll be aware of in the platform I O you can find here under libraries can search the library and can also find here some example data, we're switching back to our main cpp. And what we're doing now is we're creating some variables. We're starting by Adafruit and we are saying PMPM is our general object or global object, and then we are defining three more global variables, one for the temperature, and of course it should name float, then we have a new pressure. And as well, we have that attitude.

```
15
16  #include <Arduino.h>
17  #include <ArduinoJson.h>
18  #include "wifimqtt.h"
19  #include <Wire.h>
20  #include <SPI.h>
21  #include <Adafruit_BMP085.h>
22
23  unsigned long previousMillis = millis();
24
25  Adafruit_BMP085 bmp;
26  float temp;
27  float pressure;
28  float altitude;
29
30  void setup()
31  {
32    Serial.begin(115200);
33
34    if(!bmp.begin()){
35    }
36  }
37
38    connectAP();
39    client.setServer(mqtt_server, 1883);
40    client.setCallback(callback);
```

Of course, the altitude won't be changing here, so much about for training purpose, we're using here three data's then in the setup, we are starting the sensor and we can do that with if the BMP module delivers us and false back then we say zero print line, bmp couldn't start or could not start. And then we sang while one so this is an endless loop because it doesn't make sense that we start our sketch with out and proper module, therefore, this is an endless, an endless loop. Okay, with this, we started the module and now we can jump into the loop. And for example, every three seconds, I would like to have here the new values. So our global value variable is called temp and then we could say BMP read and it's called Read temperature. As you can see the intelligence making proper suggestion then we could say pressure is Vm pm dot read pressure and we have to calculate the divided two 100 words that we get the proper value from it, because I would like to have it in Hector's column and then we want to have the altitude is no idea is PMP re read altitudes and then I make here and function where we printing out the values so that would not spam here, our loop therefore we

85

make print sensor well you and this one could be commented then we are copied going right to the top and then we're making here on white sensor value or print sensor value.

```
39   connectAP();
40   client.setServer(mqtt_server, 1883);
41   client.setCallback(callback);
42  }
43
44  void loop()
45  {
46   if (!client.connected())
47   {
48    reconnect();
49   }
50   if (!client.loop())
51    client.connect("ESP32Weather");
52
53   unsigned long currentMillis = millis();
54
55   if (currentMillis - previousMillis >= (1000 * 3))
56   {
57    temp = bmp.readTemperature();
58    pressure = bmp.readPressure() / 100.0F;
59    altitude = bmp.readAltitude();
60
61    printSensorValue();
62
63    previousMillis = currentMillis;
64    //Serial.println("blink");
```

And what we can implement here isn't zero print. Because it's 10. But just because it's lower defined, and then we can say super print temperature and also we can add here the unit also. Then next one I have here prepared this is the pressure and that's the attitudes. And so we have here our print sensor values and this will be invoked in the loop. So let's check if the compiler has here. Something against our codes, maybe some misspelling or something else. Then we're uploading the sketch to our ESP 32 I've already connected the cable and switching to the serial monitor. And let's see, after each three seconds we should get here new values from our sensor. And we see here temperature pressure altitudes, books very good. So the first part of the mini weather station with the PM 180 I finished in the next project. We want also getting the data from the light sensor

# BH1750 LIGHT SENSOR

I'm sure also this task will not overwhelm you. So let's take a closer look on the platform in in because we need an next library.

Therefore we using the BH 175. Library. Switching back to the main cpp, and we're jumping right on top because you we have to include also, the library includes bh 3050. And then we can also your create and global object. It's called bh 175. And we're calling it light meter, for example. This is our object, then we could because we are here, making in Serial print, and we could say, for example, this will be the elimination.

```cpp
32
33  void printSensorValue(){
34      Serial.print("Temperature: ");
35      Serial.print(temp);
36      Serial.println(" °C");
37
38      Serial.print("Pressure: ");
39      Serial.print(pressure);
40      Serial.println(" hPa");
41
42      Serial.print("Altitude: ");
43      Serial.print(altitude);
44      Serial.println(" Meter");
45
46      Serial.print("Illumination");
47      Serial.print(altitude);
48      Serial.println(" lux");
49  }
50
51  void setup()
52  {
53      Serial.begin(115200);
54
55      if(!bmp.begin()){
56          Serial.println("BMP could not start!");
57          while(1){}
```

And we using here as well. And a new variable, and we call it F, we already defined the value No, we haven't, therefore, we making in fluids. And it's called Lux. That's the unit that we can close here, the data. It's called Lux. And also the variable is called Lux. Very good song. Then in the loop, we want to get here and fetch the data and therefore our global valuable, then light meter is our object, point read light level. And that's it. Then we are uploading once again, the sketch to our ESP 32. Here is the light sensor on it. So it could be that I have not sufficient illumination here on my desks. Normally it should be round about 500 Lux in an office. So I'm very curious what it will be now open the serial monitor. Let's see on what data we are getting here back and I missed something because yeah, minus two lakhs. What do we have forgotten? We should of course start the light meter. Then once again, upload it and now restart not connected. Connected and we have 800 likes, Oh, okay. Yeah, I should make once again. And as you can see, here we have our

87

data, right what we want, and in the next step, we could talk about sending the data to our no dreht

# TRANSMIT SENSOR DATA TO NODE-RED

In order to read we are getting here an inequality topic, and M Quiddity. In and we want to have you and Deepak So with these two parts, we can now set up our data transmission, double click on it, we are changing here to our broker what we have here, the 575 point point point is where our equity brokers already insert, and we're making here the weather station, for example, quality of service, I'm always taking your serum, and then we could click here finished on applying. And as you can see, with the pointy underneath the M Quiddity topic, we can see here, it's already connected. Okay, so let's switch back to our code. Now, I'm closing at a terminal so that we don't get distracted. We want to have now to send also the data afterwards. Therefore print sensor values, we could say here, sent we'll use wire em quality for example. copy it, go to the top and we're seeing what sensor will use send sensor values via M Quiddity. And now we are making an chasen. Therefore we have to make here and dynamic chasen, not buffets and document and we'll call it doc, we're making improper size. With 1024, we have the right amount, then we're saying the doc should include the temp Bucha. It's called temperature. And I've already prepared the other ones. So it's called pressure, altitude and Lux. And with these form content, we're creating also an char and buffer for the whole handling with the JSON document then we're making a civilization serialized JSON.

```
23
24  unsigned long previousMillis = millis();
25
26  BH1750 lightMeter;
27  Adafruit_BMP085 bmp;
28  float temp;
29  float pressure;
30  float altitude;
31  float lux;
32
33  void sendSensorValuesMQTT()
34  {
35    DynamicJsonDocument doc(1024);
36    doc["temperature"] = temp;
37    doc["pressure"] = pressure;
38    doc["altitude"] = altitude;
39    doc["lux"] = lux;
40
41    char buffer[256];
42    serializeJson(doc, buffer);
43    client.publish("weatherstation", buffer);
44  }
45
46  void printSensorValue()
47  {
48    Serial.print("Temperature: ");
```

And we're seeing here the doc and the buffer those two elements
will be serialized and now we can publish the data to our wire and
Quiddity to node read and hear on the topic which we are already
declared here weather station and then we could add here the
buffer elements okay because here the values the chase value will
be transferred in the buffer element and then it will be here sent via
M Quiddity. So let's see if this works so far. Uploading the sketch
and then we should see the connection from our Wi Fi and encoded
a program. And each three seconds we should get here the data in
the debug console. And here we go. And as you can see, the JSON
is perfectly format formatted and were few the temperature and
pressure altitude and the Lux values in in float volume. And later on.
We can work and edit in the node ret.

# SAVE DATA IN INFLUXDB

First of all, we have to install the influx DB node, we go to
installation in flux dB. And then we're using here the node red
contributed in flux dB. If we have already installed it, we can search

it on the left side, in flux dB. And for example, we can use the influx DB in nodes. Or rather use the influx DB outs node, then double click on it. And now we can hear make your some installation. And before we can do that we have to get here. Also, for click here, we need a token. Where do we get this token, we can click here on our instance, from influx stubaier, mostly with the part 8086. And we can go here on the second menu point of API token. And then we can create a generate new API token custom API token. Then, for example, we have here the bucket No, read what we already installed. Click on Generate. And now we're getting here and token, this token will be copied to the clipboard. Let's see if it works. Yes, no reds, then I'm creating here new influx dB. It's from the version two. Then I paste in the token, the address will be HTTP. But with the port 88. Six, then it's called influx dB. Then we saw not verify the server certificate because we haven't any SSL certificates. Then we click on add the organization. Let's see what do we have here in the organization members about the organization it's called pixelate. In my case, the bucket is not read, you also can see that here on buckets. That's the node rates you also can create some new buckets and the measurement.

This is what we are entering now. And we say linear weather station for example. milliseconds, it's okay, we click on Finish. And then we could say yeah, deploy. Let's see if everything works. Looks good so far. And now we can connect our chasen elements directly to the influx DB node. Then we click on deployment. And now we are ready, saving the data into our influx DB P. Let's see how can we find them we are switching back to influx dB. Let's take it here so that we can see both of them. Then you'll be getting the fresh data, we click here now in Data Explorer. Here's our bucket. It's called not read until we can search the measurements what we already insert here used to mention it and it's called mini Weather Station. Here are the four elements what we already insert. And then we click on Submit. And here is the visualization of the four well is very good. And when we click here on submit, we always already get in here the new data can see here the past 15 minutes that we see a little bit more past one minute. As you can see here. We are from perfectly dashboard with our fresh data. And here you can see temperature 22 degrees, the bottom and this is what we want for later on that we can work with this data also in Carvana.

# VISUALIZE DATA IN GRAFANA

Now let us make the Grafana integration before we open Grafana. Normally on Port 3000, we have to log in. And then we checking under Settings Configuration. And we're making here the data sources. Here is already an influx DB insert. And I'm showing you how you can add another InfluxDB InfluxDB. Here is the URL what we are using, as before. But first of all, we have to change it to Flux that's really important, then, let me see do we have Yes, including the port, the port, then no basic authentification, the organization it's called clicks to add in. And then we have to add here a new token. So let's see an API generate new API token, custom API token buckets, only the node Read, read and writes generate a copy this one because this button doesn't work. In my case, then we insert the token. Then we setting the default bucket to a node read I think, and then let's see if it works. We call it influx dB. And other name, safe and test. Data Source updated data sources work in one bucket found, if you have here any troubles, then take a closer look. If you have here something entered in the authentification. Or maybe the token is not as it should be. And now we have access to influx DB via our Grafana. And now we can make for example, a new dashboard, click a new new dashboard.

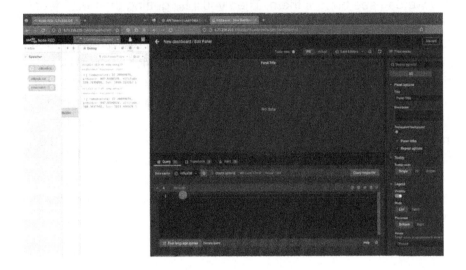

And could say here, for example at the new panel. And now we have to add to the InfluxDB data. And no worries, we just click on Data Explorer, as we did before, click on Submit. And now we can change the script editor. And with the Script Editor. We just copy this query, pasting in here the query. And what we can do now is here we want to filter for example, if I only want the temperature, then I get rid of the last of everything behind this line. Then let me see if this works. Then we say for example, query inspector, refresh, it looks good. And here we can see the data, the actual data which is coming here. Then we can add here for example, the panel title, temperature then let's call it a bit down here the graph for example, filled with opposite team then I would say here the last five minutes, then I could see radiant mode a little bit different. The point says let's put it up unit Celsius let me see if we have here some socios for example. And of course you could change here a lot more of the things I click on Apply. And now I have in my dashboard here the temperature values what we are fetching, let's see the temperature 2222 for 22 Six last minutes, then we say for example, every five seconds, I would like to refresh it. So we can see 27 Getting Yeah, the fresh data 22 720 to seven perfect and this you could do also with the other parts. That means we could add here a fresh panel then we could paste pasting in the the query from before and now I would like to have the pressure for example. And the pressure I don't want to like here and chart and therefore we could change it to time series for example, in an Gulch applying then we could change the size of the Gulch this so you have here and very nice possibility for a dashboard and you also can go to in cyclic view mode and then only in full screen you see really nicely what is going on in your room and as you can see the sun is shining right now and her room temperature will increase very very fast because the sun is directly shining into him the sensor and this is why the sensor temperature will be increasing. Yeah, slightly

# CONTROLLING A FAN WITH MQTT

In this project, we want to start and stop the computer fan with the ESP 32. Therefore, I've connected the ground and the plus from the fan to the GPO 18. And then we can start it via M Quiddity. But therefore, we have to add an M Quiddity out. And to inject notes for example, one and two, the inject notes will send us an Boolean for example, true. And he also Boolean but I would like to have your false and then we call in here the topic fan. Choosing the proper M Quiddity. Server, coolers zero retain is false. Then we are connecting both injects to the topic. And now we can send True or False to the topic fan. What we have to do now we have to change the Wi Fi M Quiddity. And in the function you're in the recollect, we have to subscribe to the topic fan. Now the ESP 32 is listening to this topic. And if now we're jumping to the callback, and if we're getting the topic fan, then we can do here something that means we could say here if the message temp and this is what we are getting here. This is the message temp. If the message temp is true, then something should happened. And else also something should happened. And as you can see here, this isn't string. Why is it in string because the topic is in pipe message and will be translated or converted into an char, for example, or an in string. And therefore, the Boolean which were sent from not read to our USB is now an string. So but we haven't got declared here any thing from our fan in the main cpp and therefore we're changing to our global section, and we're seeing your bytes. For example fan is on the pin number of GPO number 18. And that we can use it we have to jump into the setup part. Here we go. And you could see here the pin mods for the fan is output. And I'm putting this right under the server begin. And now we can change back into Wi Fi and Quiddity. And we could say for example, digital rights fan height if it is true, and if it is false, copy, paste and we're seeing low let's check if everything is right. No, yeah, we have no excess off the fan. Why is that so because the fan is declared let's let's see the fan is declared afterwards, we reference the Wi Fi and Quiddity the Wi Fi and Quiddity is at the runtime already referenced and then the fan will be declared to get rid of that we can copy this and could say in the Wi Fi M quality for example x or paste it in and then we could say x term with these power meter, the compiler knows AHA the variable fan will be referenced or declared later on in the code.

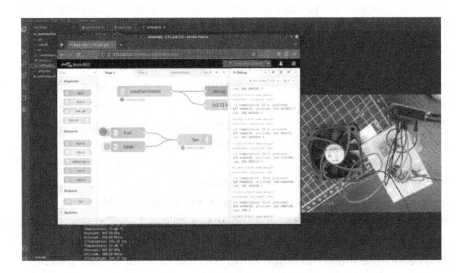

And now we can fear and clear signal then we are connecting back our ESP 32 and upload the sketch then everything is connected so we are getting our fetch data each three seconds then let me show you also this one and then a lot of windows now are open so that we can see a little bit more than I'm clicking now on true and the fan is starting and as you can see, in the meantime we are getting the values from via M quality sent to our M COVID-19. And during this session also can send out and quantities now and clicking on false and the fan will stop and this is What I would like to show you in this short example, that we can send data via JSON from the ESP 32 to our node, right? And also that we can send out your things and we can use here. Normally in real time. Our use our modules like to fan young with em Quiddity

# CONTROL FAN WITH HYSTERESIS

In this project, now we are talking about hysteresis. It's an to point controller. And think about when we have a we want to control and fan or an air conditioner. And we have here and diagram on the x axis is that the time and we have the temperature in degrees Celsius. And for example, the red line is our temperature. And when the temperature is moving from 18 degrees Celsius to 27. And when 27 is our, for example, in red, we're catching the data making an F, and if it's above 27, the fan will start it and then the temperature or will cooling down and after the 20 or below 27, it will shut down the fan and then the temperature will be increasing once again, and so on and so on. And when we have just a single line that 27 degrees, the fan will be turned on and off in very, very fast time. And this is not what we want. And hysteresis. For example, in this case, we have here and call it or from two, for example, degrees, that means if the temperature will increase to 27, nothing will happens when it creases and goes above 29 degrees Celsius, then the relay or the fan will start it. This is indicated here within one, then the temperature normally will be cooled down in the room. So the temperature will decrease. Under 29. Nothing happens because we are in this corridor, it's 28, it's 27. And when it comes below the 27, the relay will shut down. And then the temperature will go heated up again.

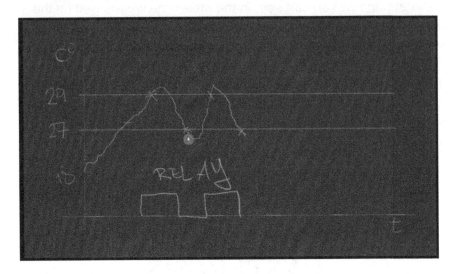

And it's increasing again and again. Above 27, nothing happens. But when it increased or is above 29, the relay started all over again. And this is a normal process for heaters, for example. So that it's not just clicking on and go off and on and off and on. And how can we do that in the not read, we could install here a new note. It's called hysteresis. Now what contributed hysteresis, install it, and then we can find it here. And what we can do now is for example, I'm inserting here for the purpose and inject node with the number and I would like to have your 25 then I would like to have your 28. And I would like to have 32 for example. Then we are connecting these three values. And normally these values will come from our temperature sensors, but that we can test it here now a little bit better. I've included here the includes or the in in check nodes, then I'm adding in debug Note that we can see what is happening and also I would like to have here the event later for example, then so now, we are want to edit the hysteresis. Let's talk a little bit in double click the threshold is in fixed one and like we have discussed before, I would like to have the above the upper threshold to 29 and the lower threshold to 27 degrees and then we could say your upper threshold should be the original message. Let me see. It should be untrue. And the lowest Rathod should be and false. Because when the threshold is above, then I would like to have been true that the ventilator the fan is going on and above. I would like to have been false that the fan will go out. Then the original topic is okay. We click on Finish deploying, then let's see if it works then turn on the code is the same because we are just sending to the M Quiddity. And true and false. This is what we do with with the hysteresis and this is also one main advantage of no read. We included here now in logic and we don't have to We'll edit the JSP code. So let's see, I inject here and 25 Nothing happens.

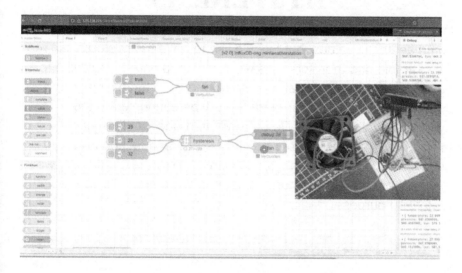

So now I close the debug for the purpose, so that we can see all of the deep x 25, nothing happens 28 Nothing happens because we are in this corridor. It won't go on, as you can see here, but now, we are having urine the upper threshold, and therefore when we are clicking 3231 30, etcetera, then the hysteresis will give us an A true let's see, and it's go on perfectly. Now, we are simulating that the temperature will be cooled down. And therefore for example, we are going back to the temperature it's near everything near 28 For example, and as you can see, nothing happens because we are in this corridor, and nothing will happen. Now it goes down goes down, for example, it is now on 26.5. We are clicking as you can see the fan is already on. We're clicking on 26.5 It's in low band, it's underneath, and it goes down. Now, once again 28 Nothing happens. So 32 It's up. And when it's jumping right to 26. Of course it's go down. And this is a two point controller, also called hysteresis. And within relay and an air conditioner for example. You can control it very easily with no red and an ESP 32.

# TEMPERATURE VALUES AND HYSTERESIS

We are not finished yet, because now we are just simulated with some aesthetic values, but I would like to have the hysteresis in real life example and therefore, this we could keep here I would like to have here the weather station data from our we have it clear and deploy now, that at this temperature will be connected to the hysteresis that is the real life data will start and toggle my fan therefore, we are using here and let me see and faction notes because we are getting in chasen with a lot of datas and I only want to have here the temperature value. And therefore, let's see debug for testing purpose.

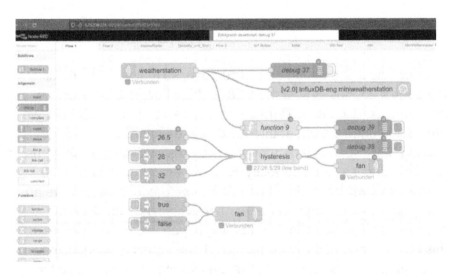

Then switching off this debug and we are adding here dev function note it is function or we are creating a new variable it's called temperature and this is nested in the message payload in the temperature as you can see here, it's in the first area temperature and here I gutting getting here a lot of commerce therefore, we say to fixed to and so, only you should have here and that is value, then I say message payload I override it is temp because otherwise I will get the whole JSON This is not what I want. And now, let me see him 22 Eight perfect this is exactly what we want to have here only the temperature value and these temperature value now, we could handle directly to the hysteresis. So therefore, connecting here. And as you can see here, low band because 22 Seven, nothing happens. If I start now, the ventilator the fan, it will be immediately turned off because we are triggering the hysteresis the lower points. Very good. And now with this little faction, we have implemented our minivator station with saving the data to our influx dB, controlling it with a two point controller with an hysteresis and also manually started because this is also working. Nevertheless, if the hysteresis is working or not, we can turn it on and off manually.

# VISUALIZE WEATHER DATA ON THE E-INK DISPLAY WIRING

Let's start with the worrying part. I have the EP hat from Reisha. It's a 2.13 inch epaper display. And as you can see here, it's it has here a pin and GPIO pin header for the Raspberry Pi and but it also can be used perfected with an Arduino and with an ESP 32. In this case I'm using the little seed studio Chou, ESP 32 C three because later on I would like to use it with a battery and this small USB as the battery management on board so it's very easy to plug and play with LiPo battery and also you can recharge it over the USBC port from the ESP 32. And the connection.

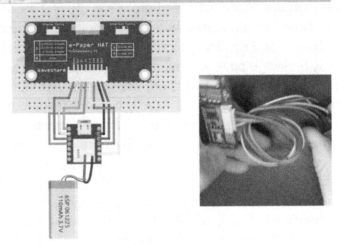

Normally there are fixed ESP 30 twos with an E Ink but in this case I really like it because you can operate it with jumper cables and you don't need an fixed USB attached to them, ie paper hat. And let's see what the connection says. You use the SPE ports, the normal SPE ports from the ESP 32. And of course you can use another board as well. And as you can see here, you connect all of the ports what I've mentioned em and later on we are also describing in the constructor, the other ports UPS besides the SPE ports and also on the serpent's rewards will be powered through the USB and because it doesn't need too much of current ground and as you can see all the other will be here connected to the USB port. And once again as you can see here the jumper cables will be attached here directly to the ESPN and in the next project, we will see the reference in the court.

# PLATFORMIO AND XIAO ESP32

We started this project by setting up now, the ESP 32 C three from a seed studio. Therefore, I'm using here the basic sketch what we defined here later on going to the platform IO. And here I have the documentation from the platform I O dot, O R G, and it depends on what kind of USB keyboard you're using, you can find here all the proper information, so copy and paste it. Then I'm using the Arduino framework, the speed will be the same. Now I'm locked in a year the ESP 32. To check what the port is we go to Import device.

And it's actually one that I have to change where we are here and that that doesn't work. Once again, the wise Here we go. Copy Paste. And now we can insert here the ports. Then let's check back here on the main cpp we have our blink inside let's upload. So to sketch is already uploaded, then I'm on the camera. Here's the schedule the finished project was on. Therefore, there is something on the E Ink now I'm restarting the ESP 32. And codec is connected Wi Fi is connected and we have here the blink. So first initial test is successful. That means we have implemented our ESP 32 in the project. And also with the Arduino IDE. Switching back here and the full screen, you can go to data to the settings. And here in the body rules you have to enter here. This will URL with GitHub content expressive and it needs the Deaf index. And with the Deaf index, you can have Yun click on key when you install the ESP 30 twos, then you can find on the board's ESP 32 You can find the SAO or let me see where is it so ESP 32 There we go. And then you can as well upload the contents to the seed studio via the Arduino IDE.

# E-INK HELLO WORLD

Let's start with an minimal example. And therefore we using the library, g x EPD tufan gene Mark thing, you also get this in the Arduino IDE. Therefore, we click on it, click on installed and what we want not that was not right. Once again, cheeks VPD tune. Then on installation, and I want this entry copy, go to our platform in en, and we have here this one, when we compile it, then the library will be downloaded and this is what we want because we want as you can see all dependency with the Adafruit GFX etc, will be installed. And now when you're in the Arduino IDE, you can go into examples and find the example from this library, we have to go here into p i o. And now after check is it lip depths, CH studio on GX EBT X samples. And here for example, we have the minimum example. And here we have the inner then I split it to the right. And we open our main cpp. And now we can choose here, whatever we want, and can build up our own example with our basic sketch.

And this is exactly what we want to do. Now, first of all, we want to include here at the very first beginning of our basic sketch yearned content from the Chi x eptb, we and it's really seem This is here, and I can get rid of the includes some, this is what we want to have here. And now we want to select the proper constructor. And, and the proper constructor will be find also here on a display selected new how's it called a new style, age, then we also split this to the right. Once again to the right. And here you can find a lot of constructors regarding your size of the E Ink display. And here you go through what you have. And then you can paste in the proper constructor. In my case, it's this one up where's my cursor, here's the cursor. And let's see what we have here I have 2.1 a three inch therefore, I have also declared here that the CS pin is on number five, as we can see here, this is the cspn then we have the DC pin on chibios. Two, three and a Basilan on phone the rest is s it on isn't under SBIR. This is what we need for the construction. And yes, it's in the display section. Okay. So far, so good, then we can jump back to the minimal example. Because this is what we want to do now, we want to now also declare here and in general global scope and char which is called Hello world, because the first part is also always in hello world that we have here. And now in the setup as we can see here, we want to have here that display in it and also copy and paste here all this stuff and we are not putting it into the setup. Because I would like to have here and hello world minimum function and in this function we can post the everything in from this stuff. And here we are not posting I'm printing out and static. While your we would like to see your display dot print. And it's called the Hello World from above, this one will be referenced here. So what we are doing here we initiate the display set the text color is black it's I have only one color and this is will this is the function that we have here our minimum example. So what we do now is after the A connection will be made. We are starting our Hello World minimum example. But I would say not afterwards. Let's do it right away. And the loop doesn't affect us now just giving out some blinks. That's all what we want to have now. So then uploading the sketch

# ALIGN TEXT AND ADJUST FONT

In this example now, we want to change the font and the text in rotated way, so that we can have here and fullscreen. Therefore, we use our sketch from before and now we are adding a few lines of codes. First of all, we will entering here a new font, and this font is will be referenced from the Adafruit g f x data, and Adafruit GFX will be referenced also when we are including year, our library you can see it here on the lip depths seed studio ECRC, the Adafruit GFX. And when you're consulting or can Google it, there are a lot of different fonts available. And I'm using yarn this 9.7 Bolt free mono font. And then here we go in here on the Hello World minimum example. And first of all, we get rid of the static value because later on we want to pass the values via equity team. And so we preparing here and parameter, for example, using text and this ink text will pass to the display print. Don't forget, we invoke in the setup here the function so we have to pass here string hello pics lady, for example. And now here after the init we want to say here display dot set, I think it's rotation and we rotate it to one side its horizontal, then we say Display set font and we reference the three mono what we are F here it's called the free mono Boyd's seven stuff that should be working also as well. And next thing is we are creating helper variables. And these variables will now be calculating our display text that we get the bounce we are inserting entering the text and nevertheless how long it is we will getting back the bounds of the text and this will be very beneficial for us because now we could say calculating the start and end point from the dimension of our display the width and the height. Why am I copying pasting this this is also one of the examples in the library.

Then we could say Display set of full window and the text color as well. That's it. Now we're on the first page and in the first page we can see now your filler screen that's okay but now we have to say set the cursor and we have here our x and y values Okay, sounds good to me him so let's see if the compiler throws us any error this looks also good. Then I would say we are trying out now there are uploading the sketch started all over again. And there we go. We have the texts in the right way with a little bit bigger font.

# CONVERT AND EMBED GRAPHICS

Now we want to add ear and photo, our graphics to our eight inch display. And therefore I've already created one. And this will be in the background and later we override with text here and the data from our API, for example, your degrees Celsius, which they will do we currently have, and here's the forecast. And this is just a normal GPS and JPEG data. And this JPEG will now be translated and converted into a byte array. Therefore, we using this site, we are uploading the JPEG leave everything in the normal meta, because the JPEG isn't the size of my ink display. So I have not edit here something.

Then later on, I go on, generate code. And I can copy and paste here, this output, what we can do now, we are creating here in our source folder, a new file, and we name it a in image dot h and copy and paste here. The thing from the website, delete the last one, jumping to the top because I want to change here. The name, as you can see is a lot of data inside. That's the reason why we change it here to extra header file, save it. And that's it. Nothing more to do here. No worry about this red underline. This is the intelligent IntelliSense from Visual Studio code. When you compile the code, everything is fine. Okay, jumping back to our main cpp and now we want to show just the raw data, the raw image data. Therefore, I get rid of all of the funds now because what I want to do here is this plan dot draw, and it's called inverted a bitmap from 0x. And y is on a zero because I've fullscreen, then the name of the byte array, it's called a Inc. Image I was called image. Then we have fear 250. That's the size of my ink display. And I want the color. It's EP D black, yes. Okay, the rotation, we get rid of it. And we say here display fill screen, for example, with a white so that everything will be deleted if something else is on the on the screen. So Inc image isn't recognized. Because we haven't got insert here. The header data does include the image dot h. That's the reason why I got any suggestions before. And here in the display. We can say get rid of it. And display fill screen and so on will be come here in this area. Looking good so far. Let's check if the compiler goes along. Looks good so far. Then we say Display set rotation what we delete before but we need it here on display set full window. Looks good. Now we have here the first page and that we can also get rid of and we could say your next page. Yes, upload the thing. Let's see if we are right here. That's our previous sketch. Then let's see. And there we go and refresh. And here is the image from before in full screen. Let's see if we can get it here a little bit closer. Perfect. That's all what we want for now. And in the next step we will add some text

# DISPLAY TEXT AND GRAPHIC TOGETHER

So far we have embedded the the graphics and displayed it correctly. What we want to do now is to get here on the right and text. And we know the coordinates here are 0.0, we have 250 pixels and 128 pixels. And this is how we could now at some aesthetic text, okay, therefore, we jumping into our tool while from the display, we have already filled the screen with white, and then we are displaying the bitmap graphics. Afterwards, we want to add some text. First of all, I would reference here more fonts. So this thumb thumb is a very, very tiny one. This is just to visualize you how tiny we can fill out here some text. And this is an normal font. But I would like to have here my text, okay, and for the static text, we say Display. Set font, and it's called the free scence. That should be right, then we are adding and display a set text color. And this will be an GXE, P and D are black. Then as the next point, we are now setting the cursor, and there's a little bit trial and error. But I think this could go along certainly 60 and 35 in y and we see here display dot print. And I'm printing out the value, for example for the temperature 25. So next one, we are copy and pasted display set cursor 60 and 95. It's cloudy that's underneath. And then I have here something prepared. We are setting also the next are the same font, maybe we won't like to change it. Then text color once again, set cursor 172 30 170 in the x axis and then underneath so that we get here to the Columbia symbol. And there's for example Thursday.

Then, underneath, I change the text size, the font size to an very, really tiny one. It's 170 and 14. And there is for example, some data so that we know what date is in our forecast. Okay, let's upload it see if it works or if we have to change and adapt to some kind of the cursor. Looking good so far. Now it's uploaded, and it's changed perfectly. Let's see what we have done now. And as you can see, we have now here the 25 the temperature we have here Thursday, and it's here cloudy, exactly what we want. And once again in the years to part of the 2560s 35 underneath with 60 and 95 for the same list, the text cloudian the web Thursday with a tiny text attached.

# WEATHER DATA REST API

Now we want to have service and API where we can fetch actual, better data. And therefore we using Open weather map, or CI. And I know it's not the accurate, it's not the precise values. But we are just simulating here, an API call. And for that reason, it's free of charge. And you can use it. Also in your projects. Therefore, you're creating here and free. Use them. And then you can go here to your name and to your API keys, and then you'll find, then your key. But here is an important advice. When you're re registering your user, you have to need at a minimum one hour. When more. Also, it's possible that you have to wait a little bit longer, then the API keys are not working instantly.

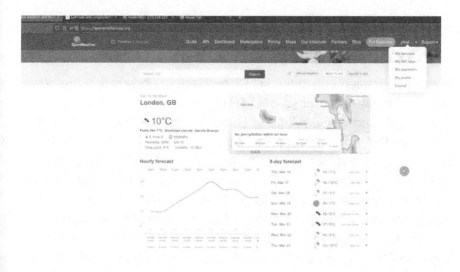

Therefore, it could be possible that your API calls are not working right away after you have logged in. So then we go to API. We scroll down a little bit down into current meta data, click into API doc. And here we go. Here we have our desired API. Hit HTTP requests. So what we need now is at the first point, and latitude and longitude, where do you get it if you're on geocacher, and then you already know it. Otherwise, you can use for example that long dotnet and then you give type in here, your place to be protected. That's not true. That's not true. Let's see. Then for example, it's broke my place. Here we get latitude and longitudes. Then once again, London you have or your adjust can pick it as well. With this data, we're setting in your longitude, latitude and longitude in the app it is of course our key what we are gathered into our panel. So we can copy and set in here our data this is for my destination. I also added here units and metric so that I have here the proper values and then I click enter and in Firefox, I already get an proper formulated chasen use the row data and here the proper station when I'm getting rid of the units. Then you can see I get here are my spinners and find height. But for me, the metrics will be is more suitable. And that's it. That's our first step that we can make here an HTTP request via the browser. And later on, we will implement it in no dread

# USE REST APIS IN NODE-RED

Now we're implementing the HTTP request. In node red, therefore we're searching according to HTTP request, then we add in here, inject, and second inject, I need some debugs. Debug debug, and I also want the n m Quiddity. Out. Then zooming a little bit in, what we're doing now is, we want to make here the HTTP request. And I want to have here also and Deepak for that. Here, we're just making the connection we come to it later. So in the inject, note, the timestamp is it's, it doesn't matter what the content is, because we just want the trigger here and the flow on the HTTP requests will copy our URL. It's an GET method. And we seeing here let's see, two callback is supposed to chasten that looks good, the payload will be ignored, because it does matter what we are sending here through I just want to call back, we click unfinished. And here I have to type in something that I don't get me an error just as a placeholder.

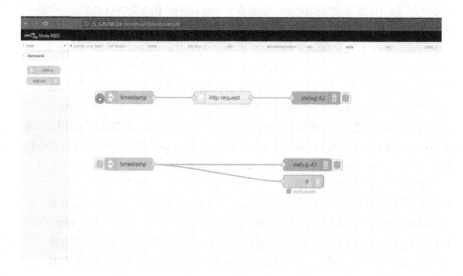

Then we are switching into our debug Node and now we are making the HTTP requests. Let's see if something comes to us. Yes, here we have now and proper valid JSON data of all of the things from our HTTP requests. What we are doing now is so that we can prepare here and good Deepak situation that we copy this chase now and give it into an aesthetic chasen because here we have some limits and when we are testing, it could be possible that we reached the limit, the free quota limit and therefore we go in here to copy him. So I copied the static JSON, we go to timestamp. We are clicking here. For example to string pasted in finished let's see if it works. That's what we want to have. And as an encoded the out we are seeing a link for example in this topic will be subscribed from the ESP. So when we click on that we getting here and JSON data and later on we just met here and connection and we are ready in our production. But for debug debugging purpose we're using yet and static chasen

# JSON EDITING

The next step will be that we don't want to have all of the data from the JSON. And therefore we are adding here, function nodes. And within this function node, we want to change here, a few things. Therefore, the functional comes in front of the inject node, and then we are connecting you the debug and the ink in the function node. Now, we can access of course, all of the data from the JSON data. And this is executive what we are doing now, we're making here some variables, and we are accessing the things on the JSON data with message dot payload, then the first key parameter will be main bits here. And then the second parameter will be temp. And this is what we're getting out when we are accessing. So then we would like to have a new message object. And we want to have here a new message dot payload. equals, and now we could say new message dot payload dot temperature equals to that value from above the temperature. And this could be done now with a lot of others.

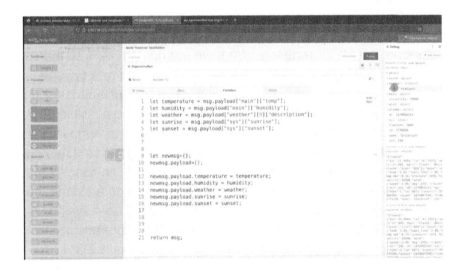

So I've prepared it. So I feel the humidity and the weather has an also let me see where we have weather. And there is an object nested for we need here and zero and then with the description, few clouds. And I would like to add a new message payloads, dot them, for example, and also New Message paid loads, date. And here, we could say, the days for example, Aetna, we say a number because later on, we will access it, we're an array. Okay? Then we have one point. Let's click on Finish, and deploy it, get rid of it. Let's see, are we have one mistake, and the mistake was in the inject note, we have to change here from string to JSON, of course, finish. And now when we inject the static response from the HTTP request, now we are getting here, our function not right away, because we returned the, the message but not the new message. So let's see if it now works. How are we there we go. Here we have our own created object with the data what we want to deliver. And so we also can process here, JSON data in Node red really easily within function nodes, just access it, create a new message object and then we're sending and returning the new message back. And so the next step will be to process these information on the ESP 32.

# FORMATTING DATE AND OTHER VARIABLES

Before we go further on, I would like to add here the data in a more precise way, because with the Unix timestamp, and with these values, we can't really do anything. Therefore, I have here created thumb points. So I will copy it in. At the very first top, here we have an array, it's indexed zero based with the names of the weekdays. And with that, we can work later on sat all day, for example, that's not too long, then we are creating a new date object. And with this date object, we saying let me give the weekday so for example, the day object delivers us n 30123, we get wetness day for example, when we getting zero then it's Sunday and this is now in the day. So, we can say here day and I also have prepared something for the date the date will be calculated we are in Moodle one we have now the year 2023 divided in a modal of 100 we get equals 20 But the rest of this division will be 23 and this is exactly what we want to have in our short format value and this is what I did here we have unformatted the date I get the date then I want to have here an integer value of the month plus one because we get in here zero is January etc and then the full year will be calculated via the modal. So I have here and proper date in the syntax of JavaScript this will be here referenced so far, so good.

Now, next step will be that we calculating here in sunrise and sunset am the Unix timestamp into an proper I would say an improper way out that we can read it before we say let sunrise time stamp equals this one and the sunrise date will be a new date. We are referenced the sunrise timestamp because the timestamp in JavaScript will be in milliseconds and not in seconds we have to multiply it by 1000. And then we can say let sunrise is sunrise.or Sunrise de dot get hours plus double point plus sunrise underline D and then get minutes it should be I think get minutes absolutely brilliant. The same thing we could do here with the sunset. So I copy paste here the thing from the sunset we'll see attack there we go. So the right reference should be included. Let's see if we are right so far. Thursday, the correct date and your sunrise and sunset in an way we can read it in o'clock format. I want to add here one more thing and this is called the lit update function. So we get here are the hours because I would like to visualize on the E Ink display when the not what's wrong here. But one the display is updated therefore we're getting here get minutes we notice Yes. And of course we reference also here update and update and as a last point, I would like to have here and logic we will use it later on. For example, let current hour is the that get Hour. And we have fixed and variable and Boolean and if the current hour is, for example, greater than five, and the current hours are less than 23. So this is will be the, the time, then the show very should be true. And if it's in the night hours, I don't want to update my E Ink display because it doesn't matter, I can't see it anyway. And therefore, it should be stay in force. And of course, new message dot payload dot show this show. And now we have all of the functions what we need, let's test if the show variable also are correct. It's now true, perfect, let's test it. For example, if we say now, we have 1030 greater than 11 Then I should get here and false back. False very, very good. So within this corridor, time corridor, we were getting here our data and now we have finished to process all of this data then out of in the ESP 32. Once again, let us check if the correct production also works very well. Timestamp. Here we go. We got two results because here the debug 42 is here. Debug 43 is our self formatted. And here we go. Everything works as expected. We're going to our debug solution deployed and now we're ready to go to switch to the ESP 32

# ESP32 REQUESTS NEW DATA

Now we are back in Visual Studio code into the Wi Fi M Quiddity. And the first thing, what we want to do is we want to subscribe to the topic, Inc, we are going to the callback function and saying here, if the topic is async in the colpack 10, here should something happen. And what should happen is that we would like to have here, the chase processing, therefore, we're going back to the no reds. And here we have proper outputs not from the original one, the raw output, we want our modified JSON copied, go to the assistant is B 32. D serialize. Next, putting in predefine. Looks good to us. Next, Next, here we go. Copy this one, it's an absolutely no brainer. copy and pasted. And there we go. We have here our data so far, in the Wi Fi and quality here is not the inputs here we have a message temp, let me see is the outer you know, chasing is missing includes doing chasing that age. I think this is the proper writing. And now everything should be fine. Yes. Okay. Let me check. If this works. So far, Serial print line temperature, I think I make your own string out of it string temperature, then upload it.

Then we open the serial monitor on getting the blinks. And when we are now inject some data onto a static variable message arrived on topic Inc. and tear, just temperature and here's the whole thing works perfect. Okay, we're not done yet. I would like now to get the data directly into our display. And it's not a very good way to work here with the single variable. So therefore, I've created here, and global variable in and struct format. And this struct handles all of the strings, for example, it could also handle floats, etc. But in this case, it's a more really overview and more structured way. And with this a ink data, this is just a template, we can access all of these ones. And now going down, get rid of this one, we could say a ink the ink data, dot temperature, string temperature, perfect. And with this already prepared the other ones. Here I make an T date and an E and D because I'm not sure if they end date is already assigned here in platformio that we don't run in any collusions I'm rename it okay looks looks good so far. Then I say if the variable show is true, then I make here and call of the function for the ink display what we are not having so far. Therefore, we are jumping back to our main

116

CPPM. And here we have an Hello minimum function which I would rename now in show show in for example, or how can we show image we don't need your any texts. So far, we've adapted and also we get rid of this one. And now we can add it yeah, all of the content. So we have nearly done everything so far. But what we want to do now is here to access all of the data from our structure. So it's called a Inc data in data dot temperature. It's already in string. Very good. While we have access to this data, because it's in the Wi Fi and quality and at the runtime we also can access it here. Show image before we insert here everything I would like to jump Back to the Wi Fi encoded here so that we don't forget it. And we'll make you the call of show image show image is not present in the Wi Fi and Quiddity. And therefore we have to make here and external external void show image. Okay, then going back to the main parts, and now we want to have the ink weather data dot wetter then we have the ink data dot, it's the day then we have the date. And what we can do now our so prepared this one in the last row, I would like to have here also a few informations with the tiny font, resetting the cursor to the last row. And this last role included then sun set and the sun down and when it's updated. Okay, so far, so good. We have processed our JSON and also referenced it in our function which we did before. Let's see if the compiler gives us a green sign Yes, and then upload the data. Then restarting the USB and also showing you the camera. So restart that we see something attempted to encoded there. Perfect. Just changed here so that we can see something. There we go. Okay, now let's open node red, clear. Now we want to inject here, the JSON data JSON JSON is arrived. And as we can see here, it's already updated our data Thursday. Yeah, in the small one, we see the date and T are also very small. But this just for training purpose we see here when the sunset is sunrise sunset, and when it's updated on which time and we see the receipt here the forecast and the temperature. Well, so far, so good. Once again, I would like to update it, it's arrived. And we getting here, the new data so that we can see that the processing is working in a correct way. I would like to add here. For example, temperature, I'm at 15.2. Once again, injected it. And let's see a year 15.2. Perfect, the processing works quite nicely. And this is exactly what we want to do. And now it's easy, because now we can just change here. Or we can leave it for example. And now we can make a connection from the HTTP requests to real life data. As we can see here, it arrived once again. And now we have the actual data from the HTTP request from our API.

# DEEPSLEEP

The main feature of this ESP 32 Chow is that we can power it with some LiPo batteries. And therefore, we want to have you in deep sleep during all of the time because the ink display doesn't need any power, as you can see here, it's not plugged in, and the display is show some information. And therefore, we jumping back to our main cpp at the top. And we're creating a new function because this is what we reference later on. And we're seeing your white set deep sleep. And then we could say for example, your serial prints line going to sleep that we have here, some debug, then this is an deep sleep function for the channel. If you have here and other boards, you don't need this line.

And then we could say for example, deep sleep 50 seconds. And here we have microseconds, this is because we have here, the deep sleep mentioned. Okay, this is all what we want later on, we could say here, for example, one hour and each hour we get in here, the USB waking up and showing us the new fresh data then into the loop going back now we want to have here for example, the current Millis and sent once sent once it's and flag this hasn't got initialized, so we have to do it. Like yeah, we can say what we'll send once is true. And this is at the very first beginning, it's no no what no function pull send once, so when it's created and started, it's true. So that means at the very first loop, we have here and true and then we are setting here to send once of false and this part will only be invoked one time because afterwards the sent once is false in this if statement is never be true. So we could say for example two seconds and then we're getting here to fresh new data new data soon then we're making urine elsif and in this elsif we could say all of this one but st ones should not be true so it should be false. And I would like to have here after I would say 15 seconds or let's do 20 seconds and then we are setting back here the previous minutes and then we could invoke Ian to set deep sleep but be aware when you're under the bulking phase I wouldn't recommend it because afterwards in the deep sleep phase you have no access of the pots it's really annoying to find the right window etc also with this boot button therefore, I would only say here and delay further for example 10 seconds and then we could say ESP dot restart is it not restart Wi Fi encoded? Let's see we have at the bottom is be restart and then the whole thing should be at the very start and why do I do this in this logic it has the meaning because I would like to be sure that the inequality is already set up of course you can ask here if client is connected then send it etc.

```
90    {
91        reconnect();
92    }
93    if (!client.loop())
94        client.connect("ESP32Weather");
95
96    unsigned long currentMillis = millis();
97
98    if (currentMillis - previousMillis >= (1000 * 2) && sendOnce)
99    {
100       sendOnce = false;
101       previousMillis = currentMillis;
102       client.publish("getWeatherData", "Give me the newest weather data");
103       Serial.println("new Weather Data cooming soon");
104   }
105   else if (currentMillis - previousMillis >= (1000 * 20) && !sendOnce)
106   {
107       previousMillis = currentMillis;
108       //setDeepSleep();
109       delay(10000);
110
111   }
112 }
```

But here maybe there are some trouble and I have here 10 seconds time to acquire here and establish on good connection. So then we are checking here the compiler and uploads then you coat saw then everything works nicely. New data is here. restarted, new data is coming 10 seconds over. I am curious if my data limits from the API is reached very soon. And the next one and as you can see, the logic works very well. But afterwards, just keep it now. We have to edit here, not the restart. We should entering here to set deep sleep. And then we could charge adapter and battery and everything should work nicely.

# CALCULATE POWER CONSUMPTION

Recently I saw an thrown away e cigarette and these e cigarettes are often only used one time. So this is an article which you can only use one time there are no rechargeable options and then this e cigarette is thrown away. I collected one opened it and there was an 500 milliamps battery inside and LiPo battery and now I can use this one for my ink display for example I connected here then here's the display. And when we see here, I'm getting here the new information. Let's try it once again. So Zack connected it and here the on the node right we saw that there is getting the fresh data and here we go. We have the actual data with this thrown away battery.

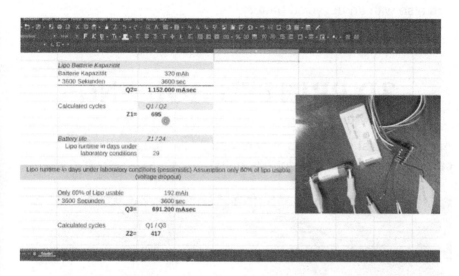

And I would like to show you what we can do with this battery. The power consumption of the ESP 32 See through Ciao fancied studio needs round about 30 seconds when it comes to the overall example with 50 milliamps that will be 1500 milliamp seconds. The rest of the one hour because I let the ESP 32 One hour in deep sleep will be in 44 micro amps converted into milliamps This is 0.044 So we have here 175 micro amps seconds. This gives us in summary 1600 and milliamps second. And with this LiPo battery capacity and I have now let me see what do we have here 550 But I say that not the whole 550 is usable because of voltage drop out and also other circumstances so I only can use 70% of it. So we have 385 milliamps hours, converted it into seconds. And so we have here the full amount of 1,000,386 milliamps seconds and now we can divide the power consumption through the whole better battery life and we have here and cycle of 836 that means if really let run 24 hours our E Ink display. Then we have here 35 days under these conditions. And this is really amazing. This is nearly a month each hour we getting updated our our whole system and if it's not 24 hours on, for example, only 15 times or 16 times a day. Then we have 52 days absolutely amazing. And when you're taking on bigger option for example, and 2000 milliamps because those are not really much expensive. Then you can see round about 190 days that's absolutely astonishing. What these little ESP can do, and also with an upcycled battery

# 3D PRINTED HOUSING

And as the last part we have here and 3d printed housing. So we can add here the display for example.

And also it has place for and 202,000 milliamp hours battery, as you can see fits perfectly in here is placed for the ESP 32 and then with your with some proper lit you can have here and perfectly fitted case where you don't need an fixed power supply and this can last over a month over two months regarding the battery volume

# SURVEILLANCE CAMERA WITH ESP32-CAM INCL. MACHINE-LEARNING NODE WIRING

And as always at the beginning, we started with the Viron part, we have the ESP 32 Cam. And as you can see here there is no use be attached to the PCB, and therefore, we need an FTD D I. And this will be our USB connection and we connect this FTDI device via UART with the ESP 32. That means the RX from the FTDI comes to the T T x from the ESP cam, and vice versa. And with these two connection, we can flash our ESP 32 can be aware, here are normally a few jumpers, and we have to set the jumper to five volts, so that we can take your VCC and Ground also to the breadboard and VCC and Ground from the ESB will also be attached. The next thing is that when we flushing the device, the five worlds from the FTDI is enough. But for the production with the web server, for example, maybe the FTDI is not sufficient enough to deliver us the power. Therefore, I'm open in the production the VCC connection, and then using an external power supply.

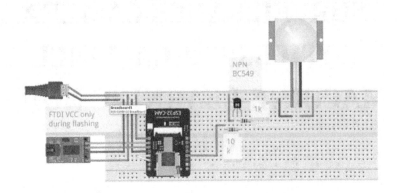

I'm not mixing your both of them because it's never a good idea to have two different kinds of power sources at once. Therefore, open up the power supply from the FTDI and use an external to have the sufficient power supply. And you will see later on what happens if we don't use an external power supply. The next point is that we have to use your jumper cable between ground and GPIO zero that we can flush the device afterwards when we are finished with flushing we have to open it because now the ESP is in the mode that we can flush it and the main sketch will not be started. Unless we open this connection restart the ESP and then the normal sketch will be started. On the right parts we have one second thing. So we only need the for the first part the left side. But for one example, we also need the second side and this right side has a motion detector and with this motion detector waken up our ESP 32 later on from the deep sleep that means we have a surveillance camera and if motion is detected, here the signal will be increased or will be amplified and the USB and got on this pin now and signal and wakens up and this is the schematic for the amplifying mode we have an NPN transistor on we have two transistor we have two resistors and we have here the PIR sensor the motion sensor. Yeah, that's all what we need for this first example

# CAMERAWEBSERVER EXAMPLE

We want to use the example from the ESP 32. And it's called the cover of epsilon. We do that because we want to check if our wiring part is everything right connected so that we can upload and sketch and also if the USB cam is working properly, therefore, I recommend using as the first sketched the example, how can we get it? In my case, I'm using the Arduino IDE to get all of the files, we click on examples, we click on ESP 32. And there we have here, let me see where is it camera and camera website. And when you click on camera observer, it will open up here this example sketch and what we need in the platform, or you can also use here as well, the Arduino IDE, but I will show you how you can do it.

It was the platform Yo, you copy these three header datas and CPP data into the main or in the source folder from your project with Visual Studio code and copy the entire data all of it and to into the main cpp that's it what we need. If you would like to go further on, then you have to change the model to to the board what you have. And then you can move forward follow me along in the platform yo we have to change the platform, anything we are using here ESP

32 cam was the expressive 32 platform, the board is the ESP 32 Cam. And we need here also the ESP 32 camera in the dependencies. Now we're going to the main cpp and at the very first beginning, we are including the underlying camera that he did, we have access all of the data, including the Wi Fi dot age. And then we can start with selecting our model. And I have fi and a camera model a I think, take a closer look here.

This is this kind of Western SD card for example, if you have an USB port, then maybe the camera model Vova kit will be changing back the rover kids model will be the best for you. So then I'm implemented the camera pins dot h and the credentials dot h the credential dot h only has the SSID and the password in it. Going a little bit down everything is from the example sketch I'm using here 1152 SuperSU. Serum and keeping everything the same. But let me see where do we have the password. Here we see the SSID and the password from the credentials. And that's it. That's all what we have to do. Then I'm switching back here I have to make the jump back connection between ground and the theorem connecting the FTDI then you see nothing blinks, then try to upload it. Of course with the proper GPIO connection. Now the sketch will be uploaded. But it won't start directly to through the sketch through things and opening the VCC connection from the FTDI because I now will give you some external power to it. And I'm opening now the sketch the jumper cables restart with the button the ESP 32 km. And now we can see the connection is made. And we can see the IP address from the web server. They open up their browser making a new let's see if the camera wraps or works. So it looks very good. Then you can see here all of the settings what we have. I'm using here 320 by 240 because I have not the best Wi Fi connection. And as you can see it's legs a little bit but now it works a little bit better. And this is what we want to do now just to test if everything works, right. And as you can see the streaming started infant surveillance camera. It's very good though What do you say it is enough what we need and you can hear play a little bit around with the special effects etc. You can also take your photos, but this was just an first test if the ESP 32 camera is via X correctly and also if we can flesh it and Linux projects we start with our practical example.

# SEND PICTURE VIA MQTT

Now we want to control our ESP 32 Cam via node ret. Therefore I'm using here, some sources from GitHub, one from this source and also from this source. And I used both of them to make here, this sketch. And now we go through it. First of all, I included here are few variables for the illiquidity connection, that shouldn't be any new for you. So here we have our encoded the server, the user, the password, and what we also have here, we taking a picture and send them picture. And these two, we now implement on Node red, that means I would like to have an inject nodes to have them. And we want to have an M code at the end out, and one in. So let's zoom a little bit in. That means, the first one, what I would like to do is Yeah, I would like to set the flesh that means should the ESP cam should use the flesh, yes or no. And also take a picture. Zero return false. Let's trigger it. And I would like to have here in the very first place, and sent send picture and the ESP 32. A will deliver a year on this topic, picture. And now we would like to see if the communication works or not.

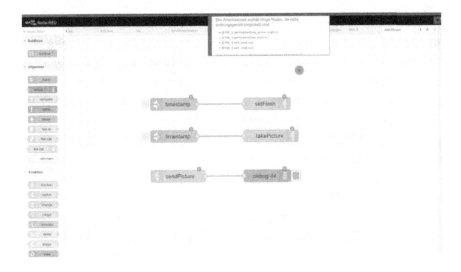

So now we have to deploy it. Okay, missing broken information. This is from another from another flow. It's not for us relevant. And now we're switching back to the ESP 32 to Visual Studio code. And what we do now is, this is also nothing new for us, we want to establish it and quality connection, I'm going to let me see to the setup. Where we have it we have to set here the pin mode for the built in LED as an output. And where do we have it? Going down down down here we're setting the M qualitat connection, the M quality server. Here we need an maximum buffer size. This maximum payloads we created also at the very first beginning 60,000. And we setting on callback because we also want to send you a set flash and take picture and therefore we need in here and callback. Then we jumping to the top because he I've implemented all of the things First of all, sent M Quiddity. The st M quality is here, implemented into the take picture. And let me see where's the take picture into the callback that means the callback is the very first function which will be invoked when the topic photo or flesh will be invoked. That means when I'm sending here, set flesh or take picture, trust and timestamp, I just want to trigger something, then here, the code will be started. So let's see what happens by the set flesh, it set flesh we are invoking and these function, we have here and Boolean, we are printing something out to flesh.

```
void set_flash() {
    flash = !flash;
    Serial.print("Setting flash to");
    Serial.println (flash);
    if (!flash) {
        for (int i = 0; i < 6; i++) {
            digitalWrite(LED_BUILTIN, HIGH);
            delay(100);
            digitalWrite(LED_BUILTIN, LOW);
            delay(100);
        }
    }
    if (flash) {
        for (int i = 0; i < 3; i++) {
            digitalWrite(LED_BUILTIN, HIGH);
            delay(500);
            digitalWrite(LED_BUILTIN, LOW);
            delay(100);
        }
    }
}

void take_picture() {
```

And then if the flesh is not set, then we are making here and short blinking array blinks not blinks beings not blinks, and we are setting the flash variable. This is everything what we're doing here, then let's see call back in the take picture, that means if we are clicking here, we trigger this flow, then the take picture function will be invoked. We have here the camera object, then we see if the flesh variable is set, then of course we are setting it to higher that means the LED is turned on. And then we're taking the picture and this is from the example sketch nothing nothing new. But what is new is that we have here and puffa. And this object where we take the picture will be taken here and also the length of it. And I feel created the function sent and Quiddity with this buffer and the length of the photo. So let's see what sent him candidatus we're printing out the picture will be sent we take a closer look if it's the maximum payload from 60,000. And then let's see the nothing happens else the picture will be sent. And here we have the client publish to the topic publish the topic publish is now the sent picture. And then the buffer link and the false variable for the Publish. And here we will get thing and zero or n one, one if it's accomplished, and zero if not, and so we getting here, picture sent 001. That's all for the very first example of our example sketch. Then, we're taking here the connection to the FTD. As we have it here, the connection to jumper cable have to be connected, then uploading the sketch right away

# DISPLAY PHOTOS IN NODE-RED

It would be very nice if we can display also a photo, what we have sent via node red or M Quiddity. In node red, therefore, we have to install your new node. Then we go to installation and we're searching for image. And it's called probably no, it's called output image output node read contributed image output, click on install. And then you can search on the left side for image and can includes these nodes into our flow.

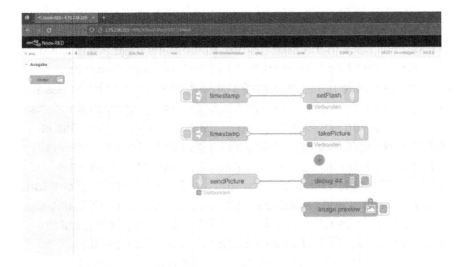

Then we have to connect here, the MQ dt in because we were sent or we get here, I take another picture. And now we getting here the binary data. So this binary data are just some hex data. For example here and as you can see, it's 24,293 arrays, and each of them array has here some values, and this will be displayed now directly here. So let's see if it works. Once again, I'm sending you a picture. So let's make my smiley face. And here we go. We have it. That's all what we want to have. Because later on we can change here, the Resize etc and can work with it and gives us some visual preview that might be usable for you. You don't need any further process. So when you have your surveillance camera, and some picture will be sent you just have to open you're not reading can see Aha, some intruders are here for example.

# DEEPSLEEP AND MOTION SENSOR AS SURVEILLANCE CAMERA

Now let us take a closer look on the variant with the PIR sensor. And we have already talked about how we could borrow everything together. And here I'm using this GPO on CBS 13 To trigger and wake up the ESP 32 from deep sleep, because this will be the perfect surveillance camera. So the ESP 32 Cam is in deep sleep and when some motion are detected, and photo will be taken and sent via an crudity to our node right in the node read. Later on, we can also send the picture for example via email or via telegram to our smartphone. So let's see we take the last sketch from before and now we made a small change so everything could be the same. But I jumped now into the setup part. We now only need the setup part because in the deep sleep it's so that ESP 32 starts all over again from initializing all barriers go to Setup and then going to sleep or whenever the deep sleep command comes. So here we're making the configuration in the Setup, then we are setting the pin mode for the LED and we are setting the frame size to VGA because I don't want to send you too much data through equity team. Then we are preparing the SD card. What's next here are we making the camera on if BT objects so that we can take a picture is to take a picture Wait a second, be turning off the camera flash and then we'll go into sleep and setting up the external wakeup GPIO number 13 going to sleep and this will never be printed.

```
219    Serial.println("Camera capture failed");
220      return;
221    }
222    take_picture();
223    esp_camera_fb_return(fb);
224
225    delay(1000);
226
227    // Turns off the ESP32-CAM white on-board LED (flash) connected to GPIO 4
228    pinMode(4, OUTPUT);
229    digitalWrite(4, LOW);
230    rtc_gpio_hold_en(GPIO_NUM_4);
231
232    esp_sleep_enable_ext0_wakeup(GPIO_NUM_13, 0);
233
234    Serial.println("Going to sleep now");
235    delay(1000);
236    esp_deep_sleep_start();
237    Serial.println("This will never be printed");
238  }
239
240  void loop() {
```

So when we start now our ESPM so let's switch to this and also that
we can see here the camera that means if I'm now the motion
detector sensor is here just catch is already open. When I'm not
putting my hand through the motion sensor, it will be taking the
picture Wi Fi connect and sent the picture as you can see here,
next one new two fingers to the camera. Let's see and picture is
sent going to sleep now. And in the picture sense take picture we're
taking the picture and here we can see taking the picture
connecting to Wi Fi and crediting them now I made a separate
function and if we are connected then we can send the buffer as we
did before through and crudity to our node right and that's all what
we need and we have here and perfect surveillance camera with
here the motion sensor once again and picture will be taken as you
can see if you are configuring the motion motion sensor right then it
will be working also through the night etc. And it will be an perfect
case for an surveillance camera.

# TELEGRAM TOKEN AND NODE-RED IMPLEMENTATION

Now we want to configure that we can make an telegram message via node red. Therefore I've logged in into telegram. And now I want to install here a few more notes, we go on installation. Then we click here on telegram. And we are using here node red contributed telegram bots. So as the next point, we can have some telegrams. And for setting up, I would suggest we go to the receiver and we go to the center. And of course, I would like to have here and debug Node as well. And now before we set up the node read part, I would like to start here with the telegram app, we are searching for the contact bot Father, this is the official telegram account for making the bots. And here we have now on Start button, we click on the start button and we get all of the lists and functions what we can do. And what we do now is we're taking in slash and say New bot. I'll write a new bot. How are we going to call it please choose a name for your bots, then we call it node red. But let's see if it's relevant. Good.

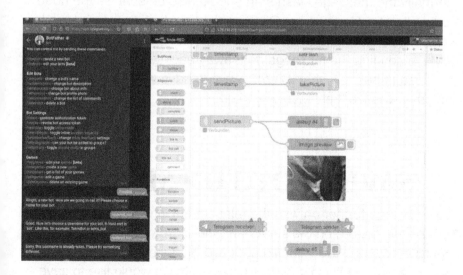

Now let's choose a username for your bots, node reds, but it's already taking place try something different node rads course but

133

for example, done congratulations on your new bot you will find it and and what else here is the API key what I want to have then we click here on Copy selected text. And now we can switch back to our node read. Because now we can edit our notes here double click on one of them and we say new telegram bot name of the telegram bot is for example node red core spot you will enter the token here you can add different users which also can attend in this chat. I leave everything as it is click on OK. Then finish also to see the telegram bot telegram cause bot and now we can make your following scenario here are two different dots we take the first one and connecting to this to the same down and also here I would like to have the Deepak so what we are doing here is if we receive here any kind of messages, then we will send it directly the message directly to telecom. So if we enter here in Word the Word will be sent via not read directly to it. This is just for training purpose. And we can see we have here connected that means then the note from regret will be connected to our telegram and the settings are right. The next step we are searching now in Telegram for our bot. Here we go we have node Red Cross but then we click on it and no message messages are here. Now when I'm clicking on Start, normally the message slash start should also be sent via the node red. Let's see. Here we go. Once again. I am testing the node red note. I'm sending this note here you can see it arrived in Node red and I'm sending the message right away back why I'm doing that because I need this chat ID etc. I want to have it for later purpose. And this was the first test ready to go.

# SAVE PHOTO ON SERVER

Before we go further on with the telecom bot integration, I would like to save the picture on the server and therefore we need here and right file note and this right file node will be connected with the send picture and Quiddity in. And this binary data we would like to save now, onto the following path. The path could be now data, USB suited to Cam and then USB so that you can dot jpg, I would like to override each I would like to overwrite each photo so that means that each picture last picture will be saved. And then also a create an folder if it not exist.

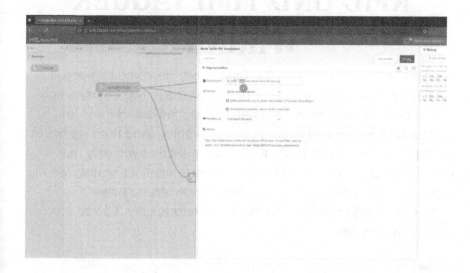

And here we'll leave it at standard. So where is this folder now, if you can remember, when we are created our Docker file, we said that our node red underline data will be linked to the internal data folder. And this is it. So we create inside the Docker container, an ESP 32 Cam folder and there on the last picture will be saved. So we'll click on deploy. Then let's start a new photo. I just triggered the motion sensor. Here it is. And now I've opened here and file tilam. So that we can see here something then I would like to refresh it. I'm already in the data from eSpin node read Yes, the node read data. And here now is the ESP 32 Cam folder. And here's the picture when we click on downloaded, and then we can open it. That's exactly what we want so that we could save the image directly to our server so that we can later on process it in the telegram or via email Notes.

# TIME RECORDING WITHT RFID UND TIMETAGGER WIRING

And as always, we start with the wiring part. Here you can see is the ESP 32 D A one is a smaller model, we have two LEDs, which should indicate us if we are logged in or logged out. Here is an resistor on from around about 200 or 100 ohms. And here we have the RFID module, he is really really important that you only use three points rewards for the model, because often it's usually we can supply five and 3.3 volts, but this device has no power converter voltage converter inside so therefore, only 3.3 volt are used in this model.

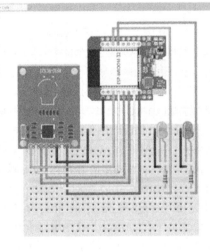

The rest will be accordingly to this schematic sta CK mostly misunderstood SPI pins, and then is the ER Q, then ground reset and 3.3 volts. This is the schematic and this one we don't use the rest will be Yeah, directly connected. And as you can see in my example, I've wired it exactly in small breadboard version here we have the module and the two chips or uncut. It doesn't matter what you have, then we can use it later on. For the practical example

# READ RFID ID

Let us start with the first sketch. And what we want to accomplish now is that we can read out the median from this chip, so that we can identify it later on in this sketch. And therefore, we have fun first test if the wiring part is correctly and also that we can communicate via aerify D with the ESP 32. And therefore, we need in the first step, and the right, the right libraries. And I have here the basic sketch as always, and I have the Wi Fi and M Quiddity connection already implemented, as we did before. And now we are adding here and library for the RF idea tool. And this called Fun MC well BWA, the M F RC 522. You can also download it on the Arduino IDE. That's all what we have to do here in the settings from the platform I own. And then we switch back to the main cpp and at the first beginning, you we have aerify dn with timetec. Some, at the very first step, we don't need the LED. We have and what do we want, we want to add to the SPI M and also their MFRC library. That's one of the first steps then we adding here the error idea text, therefore we making a const int SS pin for example, and it's 26 on the wiring and copy pasted. The second pin is the reset pin. And it's on the pin number five, and then we're creating year and a new object. It's called MFRC, five to two, but I call it RFID. And I'm passing here the two pins, the error steeping and as a spin. That's all what we need to do then, then I would like to have your two variables for the LEDs. LED green and led red.

```
13
14    */
15
16    #include <Arduino.h>
17    #include <ArduinoJson.h>
18    #include <SPI.h>
19    #include <MFRC522.h>
20    #include "wifimqtt.h"
21
22    //RFID
23    const int SS_PIN=26;
24    const int RST_PIN=5;
25    MFRC522 rfid(SS_PIN, RST_PIN);
26
27    const byte ledgreen = 21;
28    const byte led  21;
29
30
31    unsigned long previousMillis = millis();
32
33    void sendMQTTvalues()
34    {
35      StaticJsonDocument<256> doc;
36
37      doc["device"] = "ESP32 is the best MCU";
38      doc["temperature"] = random(-20, 40);
39      doc["humidity"] = random(10, 99);;
```

The red one is on 22. So what do we have ELDs. I need them Boolean for if we are checked in or not. We'll come to this later on. And that's so far everything what we need. We're jumping to the setup part. Here is something from the last part. We don't need it set up. Here we go. We are making an pin mode. The pin mode is now for the LED green. And as well for the LED red. Not led red. So far, so good. Then we make at the beginning I would say here, I'm connecting the RFID. Therefore we have to start the SP Ibis. Then Arif ID, that's the name of our object. And we say PCB, and I think it's called it is it in it? It's in it. Then we could say zero print. A rough idea? Model is ready. So as the next part, we're jumping into the loop. And here is our standard basic sketch. And we want to check if the fit is not available. Or we say it's not it's not available, it's a new cart present. That's an included function and if we are using this function, now we could say please go further on.

```
53     if (!client.connected())
54     {
55        reconnect();
56     }
57     if (!client.loop())
58     {
59        client.connect("ESP32-");
60     }
61
62
63     if(!rfid.PICC_IsNewCardPresent()){
64        return;
65     }
66     if(!rfi
67          #rintf        float rintf(float)
68     unsigne=uartSetRxFIFOFull     5();
69             =PS_RING_SHIFT
70     if (cur=remainderf          = 5000)
71     {      =MESR_RCE_SHIFT
72     previ=RECV_BUFSIZE_DEFAULT
73     // di=DR_REG_HINF_BASE        led));
74     // cl=xQueueReceiveFromISR    lo from ESP32");
75             =esp_ptr_in_rtc_iram_fast
76     }       =WIFI_REASON_MIC_FAILURE
77     }       =XCHAL_PS_RING_SHIFT
                = REENT_CHECK_VERIFY
```

And also if not the RFID. pic is it called and we say read card a
serial. Then we say return. So first basic things are implemented.
Then we have to make some helper function because we want to
read in the first step, the RFID we did. And therefore we make an
empty string. It's called content. Then we jump in the next row and
we say for now we're looping through. We have byte e i is zero. We
say less than aerify D we d size that What we want plus plus. And
now we can say, this is from the example, I copied and pasted.
Contents, concatenate, and here I'm reading the bytes from the ID
from the chip, and it will be passed to the stream. Then for example,
I could say content to upper case. Why not? And he is also an thing
from the example. And now what we want to do is, we want to
check if the content or the chip is right, therefore, I could say if
content dot substring, and that only wants to first content. If this is,
for example, such a placeholder, we'll come to it later on, then
sewer print line. Gotcha. So, then I think this is the first test what we
can do, let's check if the compiler see some mistakes, some errors,
some typing errors, yes, a lot of things to do here, then we get
switching to the illiquidity part because we don't need your any
subscription for example, we'll get rid of that. And also all of this
kind, we can also get rid of this one. Don't need it for now. And also
this one. This is a template for later on. And now we are ready to
go.

```
46      String messageTemp;
47
48      for (int i = 0; i < length; i++)
49      {
50          // Serial.print((char)message[i]);
51          messageTemp += (char)message[i];
52      }
53
54      if (String(topic) == "fromNodeRED")
55      {
56          Serial.println(messageTemp);
57      }
58
59
60
61
62  }
63
64  void connectAP()
65  {
66      Serial.println("Connect to my WiFi");
```

So we are connecting the ESP and uploading the sketch. Way too fast, we have two zero prints the RFID because otherwise, we don't see what we what the ID is from the chip. So now we can upload it again. And now we're finished with uploading restarting the ESP 32. And then we've seen Arif ID model is ready connecting to Wi Fi and everything is okay. And then when we are holding here, this RFID tag, then we see that it's reading and that's exactly what we want. We want to have here the idea and the last four points of this for example, this one for our first point, so, I hope you can see it yes, you can see it, this will be the first one this is I have the market once again. So for example, we say here this is the ESP ESP 32 Chip, then we could say S P 32. And copy and paste it then we should have an elsif. Let's do another one. So the last four for this one. Oops, too much. And this one is for example, blank. Okay, and then upload it again. Don't forget to comment out the zero prints because otherwise you got a lot of spamming in your serial monitor. Now the RFID is ready IFTT ESP 32 Tech. And we're getting there there's ESP 32 Then I have the other tech, this is the blank one. And you can see here we have the different session and before I have put on another tech, nothing will happen because we are checking here. The UU ID from digits

# CONNECTION TO NODE-RED

Now we want to transmit the data which chip is currently on the RFID reader to node red. And this is really an easy task for us because we are very well trained. Therefore we open up our node reds, then we are putting in to M crudity in for example, this is called, we could say time, and it's called use p for the first one. And here we could say for example, time, and this is the blank one. Then we add in here and debug the next debug, let's zoom in a little bit so that we can see something then we are connecting both of them. And that's it. That's all what we want to do here. And now it's connected. And with these two topics, we can send here from the loop a message and this will be done with client dot publish, then time ESPM is the topic and the message will be ESP 32 For example, then we copy it, paste it to the next one, this is called time blank and with the hashtag blank. So let's see and that's all what we want to do here.

But as we as you have seen before, if I put here, the RFID tag onto the table onto the reader, you see we won't we will spend here in the serial monitor and therefore I would suggest that we make here embed delay and of course here we can use it because I only want once when I holding it here the RFID tag and later the next second

141

the whole sketch should be stay here right at this point and then we should only get one message at the time. So let's see if this works. We uploading the sketch then we have here the node read Deepak time we have on the right side our our real time USP and and we have here this serial monitor and then I have here the ESP 32 Tech and I'm holding it in and we see no nothing entity back let's see if the blank will work. Also the blank doesn't work. Let's see where our errors oh it works but it needs a little time as I saw once again ESP 32 Blank now the blank comes with it's really laggy Arma encoded the connection wasn't wasn't good. So once again let's see if it works now. ESP 32 ESP 32. Now it works it was my ESP encoded the connection. Blank, blank, blank. Very good. Now it works perfectly USB USB. As you can see if the encoder D connection is not very well. Then it will be reconnected as in my case. And now we have also adapted here they're not read connection

# LED CHECKIN CHECKOUT

Now we want to control the LEDs according to the chips, that means if I'm putting in the ESP 32 Chip, then the green light should be turned on the indicators that we are logging in, and the blank one should be indicating us that we are locked out. Therefore, we go here to our publishing statement. And I'm getting rid of the delay because we are using that in the next function. And the function will be called toggle LED. And also your toggle led and this toggle led function I will be putting you right above the setup. Then we say what toggle LED. And now what we can do is, for example, we could check if check in this is this boolean variable the flag, if it's true, then we are logged in elsif, for example, it's not true could also use else then something other should be done with changing year the variable so that means check in is false.

```
24  const int RST_PIN = 5;
25  MFRC522 rfid(SS_PIN, RST_PIN);
26
27  const byte ledgreen = 21;
28  const byte ledred = 22;
29  bool checkIn = true;
30
31  unsigned long previousMillis = millis();
32
33  void toggleLED(){
34    if(checkIn){
35      checkIn = false;
36      digitalWrite(ledgreen, HIGH);
37      delay(1)
38    }
39    else if(!checkIn){
40
41    }
42  }
43
44  void setup(){
```

And then that's right. We say digital rights led green when we are logging in should be higher. And now we can use our delay. So that we are not sending too much information here. Then we say digital right? LED green is low. That's exactly what we're doing also in this part. Here is check in true we want to change it. Then we have here led red. And this is all what we want to do now. So once again, upload the code. And with these LEDs it's and convenient way so that you can indicate also if the equity and Wi Fi connection is enabled. For example, with some button you can click it and if it blinks blue, green, then you see it's on or not also on the start and a terminal so you don't need any OLED displays just redeem. It helps you so ESP 32 Chip. We're now putting it on. And it's red, because you're I have a second attempt. Then the blank one, the green is just so I'm not really visible. I can see it because it's cording to the resistor I think next time use red, green, red works very well. And now we have an indication if someone checked in or not. And it's not. As I told you before, when some green or some according to the chips, it's only here in this case, putting one on that means it's on putting the second time then it's red, so that means I have no indication which one that should be done yo if I'm jumping down into the sub strings. Here I could of course also indicate which chip should be used here.

143

# TIMETAGGER AS CONTAINER WITH DOCKER-COMPOSE

We are using time tiger in this practical example for tracking our time, but time taker, and I would like to introduce in our why it's such a great tool. Because the first thing what you should mention here is there's no cookie banner. privacy matters. Not only that time taker is open source, it also has an indica variants of one sold self hosting variant which we are using later on. But you also can use the old them. So for them round about three to $4 per month. And then it's absolutely no brainer, and you can track your whole time. Let's take a quick view how it's done. We can add here, for example, app demo. And then this is the demo variant. And you can add here some recordings, for example, we have your to no dread cause you do it within hashtag, then click on start. And then the time will be recorded. You can also stop it. And then could say it lasted because it's already finished till 12 o'clock. And now I have here the no dread course. And what I could do now with this hash tag is, I could say for example, what have I done this week, and I can see 100 Read costs 45 minutes, but I also had some client meeting with the client to two hours, I have client to coding and debugging and so on, you have a lot of variety, where you can track and filter whole of your recordings, you can also report it, it's just great. It's just simple.

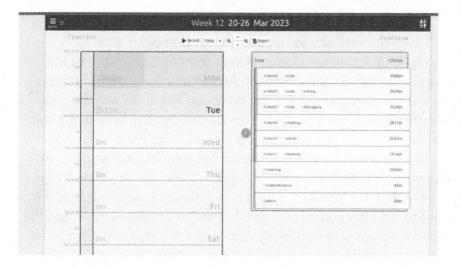

Love it. And what we do now is we want to create our timetec in an container so that we can later on use the API we are not read so that we have an RFID terminal. Therefore we are using here. Let me see. Here we go. It's on a self host. And here we can see all the things what we needing. And the thing is self hosted using Docker Compose. So Docker compose is something but we are using here and we are not using just a docker run command, we are creating an folder. So I have here and folder in our current location, user local s bin where we have our Grafana mosquito etc. Then you make here and folder timetec jump into all the time taken.

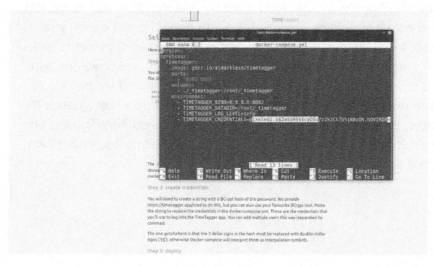

And then we are installing us the Docker Compose. With for example, up inside the Docker minus compose, you can instantly use the Docker compose variant. And what this is now all about is we are creating our own Docker compose Yamo file with nano.ca Minus compose dot yml. And enter we are creating here and YAML file. And we can copy and paste here and these lines here and be aware of the part here of the spaces because it's an Yamo file. And therefore as in Python, it's really necessary to hold here the things I've created, I've adapted here, the port to 8082. And also here we have to bind the container. The other things are the same entity, the credentials are also necessary. TimeTracker has an extra side it's called credentials we can use here for example, Excel Edie, then I'm using here no direct cause tastic 2023. Then I can copy this value, switching back to the terminal. Then we are creating here the 10 ticker credentials. And I'm deleting the existing one from the example before and be aware. We have now edit here the dollar signs because we have to adhere the dollar. This first $3 signs should be doubled up. It's also mentioned in the URI as you can see it the one got three years this $3 signs in the hash must be replaced with double dollar sign otherwise Docker compose will interpret them as interpolation symbols. Then we save it CTRL O, enter Ctrl X, and now we could say Docker minus compose up minus d for in the background. And we could start here by downloading the image. Now it will be downloaded, also extracted and now it should be soldered. So let's see if I could be my year Well, let's just check in the patina if everything works timetec locks. Looking good. Then we have at 82 Here we go, we have our app, we have to log in. No red cruise. And we are in and we can make here our first first entry in, already done. Let's do it. Let's check the locks. Everything is fine. And now we've installed TimeTracker on our server, and now it's every everything is self hosted in our own cloud.

# TIMETAGGER WEB API WITH HTTP REQUESTS

So let's try out. Now, if we can fetch data from node read via an HTTP request to our web API from time to account, therefore I'm creating here, few more texts, for example, meeting from the 830, to 9:30am. And then we have fun. Second one, we say, meeting clients, too. It's from 10 to 10:30am. Very good. Now we have three entries.

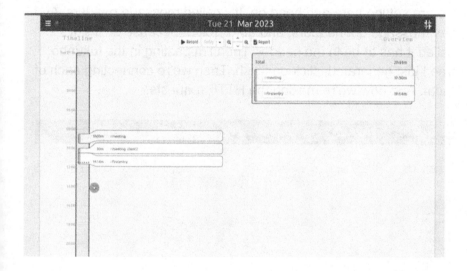

And what I would like to do now is check the support site. And we want to have the documentation. And here we can see everything about the web API, because also there is an command line tool, but the web API is that what we want. And we want to have here the first test. So we want to get the records, See below for description, the record object. So this is the tool and of course, you can use it in our self hosted variant also when you are buying here, and a normal account. So first of all, I was too fast the authentication part, API base URL, all endpoints in the API need to be attenti cated, via an odd token. And this will be getting we getting this one we are open timetec directly without any demons. Here, you have a demo on the sandbox also in your self hosted variant. And what I would like to do now is I would like to go here, on account. And here we have the API token, what I talked before we copy this one, the API token enables access to the server for third party applications, API tokens do not expire, this is really helpful. Because we don't have here any Oh of content flow with refreshing etc, reset the token revoke access for all application. Perfect. So now we have the API token, and with this URL, we can now fetch data. So then, we are needing here some inject node, then we need an function note. Then an HTTP request note and then debug not saw this will be triggered. Then in the function note, here we are putting in our authentification. So what do I mean with that? of token, therefore, we are setting here and head on. It's called message headers. And I say message dot headers, and auth. Token because so it's, it's called it has to be in the header. Then I'm pasting in the tokunbo tree I just generated, click on finish. Then we're connecting each of them. And now we're making the HTTP requests.

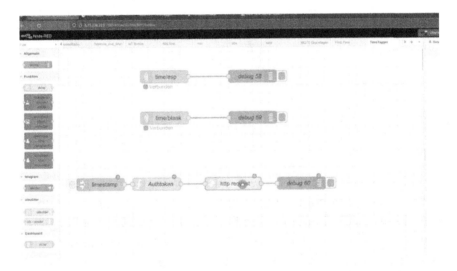

And the request will be done via get. And now we have to make here the URL. First, we have the the IP and then it should be our port. In this case, it's at 82. Then it's called time taker. As we can see here, time tiga. Then, let me see what is the next one. It's called API v2. I think it was API v2. was the first one here, API v2. And now it's going I think it was records time range, copy. Records time range, and then we need to some Unix timestamp. And let me see a timestamp. To timestamp in arrange our ego will be crew all that include the timestamp so timestamp, one minus timestamp two, we just created that one.

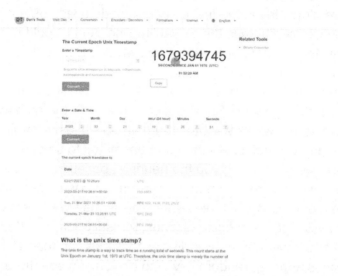

So I'm seeing here, the first one here we got minus the second one, and the first one should be the this one in the more Warning. So I would say eight, for example, just for purpose case, click on finish. Then we click here on deployment. And let's see what happens if we click here. On the timestamp, we're getting here some info, but it's not very well formatted. So it's not an UTF. Eight. It's called and JSON object. Once again, deployed, delete. Let's see what we get now. Here we go with and record with three arrays, because we already entered here, three entries, meeting meeting and first entry. So let's see. We have here meeting, meeting client two. And with the first entry, we have here, all what we want. Very, very good. And what all of the other things are keys aren't we will see later on in the API calls. But here, this was the first test if we could do an API call via no gret with auth token in an HTTP request to unofficial API of our localhost time ticker.

# PUT RECORD VIA WEB API

The next test will be if we can put an record into time ticker. Therefore, I'm deleting the first entry or I made a little bit not too long. You can see here is the actual timeline. And I would like to know how to formulate and. And object which will be uploaded via HTTP requests. But now I'm using not an get it's called input. And we just need in here, the records API. And I would like to have here and also in debug mode. So what we do now with the auth token, we copy it. And now we want to create an object just for training purpose, and this object will then be transmitted to timetec. Therefore, we are leaving you the headers, because this is what we need. And we are creating a new timestamp. So with meth for example, floor, oops, floor, new date. This is the Unix timestamp. But in JavaScript, it's in microseconds, milliseconds, and therefore, I would like to have it here, also divided to 1000s. So that we have the seconds, then an random key. And as you can see, here, we are responsible for the key when go little bit down to put records. This is the endpoint, we're getting back and accepted failed on error. And when we can go a little bit down. This is the object shape. So we need an key and unique string identifier for this record, when creating new records, it is the responsibility of the client. So we are the client and the generating the key then the record starts time as in Unix timestamp, this is T one and T two. So start and end time.

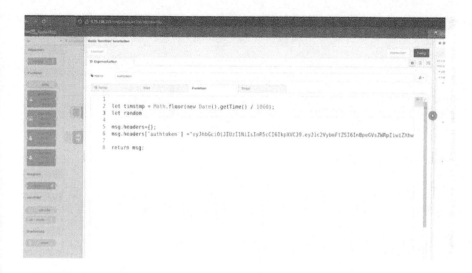

```
1
2  let timstmp = Math.floor(new Date().getTime() / 1000);
3  let random
4
5  msg.headers={};
6  msg.headers['authtoken'] = "eyJhbGciOiJIUzI1NiIsInR5cCI6IkpXVCJ9.eyJlc2VybmFtZSI6InBpeGVsZXRpLiIwiZXhw
7
8  return msg;
```

Then we have the empty is the modified time, if we update something, the record description BS, you can see the modified time and the description. And we have the server time set by the server and storing the record. This will be stored from Time Ticket itself. So what we are doing now is we want to create here and random key. And this could be done with a meth random. And I could say for example, the to string. So to six for example, and then I slice it up. And now we should have here and random key from strong enough, then we're creating here a new record. So this record has an key as our random key. And then we have time one, it's the timestamp. The time to is when the stop time, I would say it's timestamp plus 60 seconds, multiplies by 15. So 15 minutes is the record long, then we make a description. It's called from an old Rhett then I would like to have fear also, manipulated timestamp is the same one as the timestamp before, time stamp.

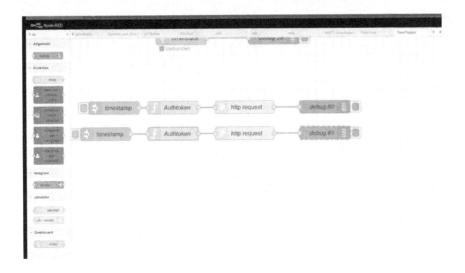

And the last entry is the server time just be via a null or and, and zero with because it's I think it's in float, no comma at the ending. And we say now this any can list it's better. And this is the new record because it's an array, as I saw before. It's not an object. It's an array, and therefore we're putting this in an array. And that's all what we have to do, I think let me see what should we do now of course, the payload should be the list. And here are the headers. And then we're returning everything. And when we have edited here everything right, then we should see a new entry with 15 minutes. So let's see if I'm doing here.

Then what do we get here we get here and accepted. This is the key what we are created. This is the key from us with this two string to the 15 times long, so I would like to add here a node one random key so that I can see the Next time, if this works, then deploy, we switch into our time Tiger. And here we go, we have here our entry deleted, then auth token, it's not auth token, it's create entry. And I would like to have here that's not read volume two, so that they can see that something changed. Once again, upload it or put it in array. And as you can see here, and this is the created value from our random Kia, what we have here, and this is also what the time ticker returns me. So we don't need this anymore. Then we click on deploy and and here we should have node read volume two. Very, very good. So we are able now to getting the last entries. So let's see. Now also, the last entry should be the volume two. It's the last one. Meeting Na, meeting client to meeting Firstly, because it's not here, because because who knows it we have entered the unique timestamp s and fixed the volume. So we have to change here. I think it was this William then deployed once again. And now we should have the actual value as well. Not really, because we are in the future, I think this is the problem. Why we set plus 15 and this is in the future so it's not it's not finished yet. Therefore, um, where's it here is it then I would say for example, I'm using year and eight. Let's see if this works. Future Time Ticket entry please show me Yes. And here we are. We have our latest time ticker Volume Two here it is very good. So as you could see, here we getting also the deleted ones so be aware here it's called Hidden from not read with this hidden description, because timetec doesn't delete any entries. It's just hidden. And as you can see here, we only have four entries, but we getting five because of the hidden elements. So we are able now to getting all of the entries and also putting entries into time ticker by not read

# USING A FLATFILE FOR SAVING CHECKIN ON SERVER

We are creating this example now in many different steps. First of all, I would like to store this whole entry in into an flat file. This is the reason because we are responsible for creating the whole entry. And as we saw in the web API, we could go is going on two different ways. The first way is that we are storing the value the future time, just by a random value. And when the person locks out, then we have to update the entry. So what I mean with that is, now I'm putting in, for example, this is the ESP 32 tag, I'm now starting to work on the ESP 32. Now I'm locked in, I've saved the file now on the server. And now I'm finished working on putting the next time the ESP cert to take on and now the record will be uploaded, in the meantime, it's stored onto the server and this is what we wants to accomplish now. And therefore, we are using here the equity out and I'm disabled now this one because I don't want to see it anymore. And now I would like to have here and right and I copy and paste the Create entry am we writing down and I would like to have here and Deepak So, this will be the first challenge. So, when we are putting here the blank chip into our fid reader, then the flow will be triggered.

And we are creating here an entry and the entry is nearly the same as we did before. But I would like to have the description as well to this description is the message payload from their chip, but we transmitted so therefore we are saying here that our inscription is now the hashtag. Description and everything else could be leave as it before. So the message header. I'm skipping here because this will be needed afterwards. And I think that it will click on finished we click on write file. And now we have to declare where we want to save this file. And we have here in Docker compose as you already know. And we are saving this into the node red folder. And so we have here the Data folder. And then we are seeing for example, time records. That's the exterior we overwrite the file. And we want to create if it's not there. Okay, I'm finished. Then we click on Deployer. Now what we want to do is I would like to have the blank chip. Let's see if this works. We see here that something will be on our monitor. That means that we have already saved it. So let's check it if it's already on the server. Therefore I'm switching to the node red folder. Then I'm jumping into the node red folder. And we should hear Ah, here it is time records to extend. And there we go. We have here our JSON file. It's embedded in an array because this is what time taken it with all of our files perfectly. And as you can see here I've already make an future timestamp 42 And in the next project, we will put out then the the entry into timetec If we add here and the button the chip a second time

# SEND RECORD TO WEB API

So the whole idea is when we already created and file, then we know, aha, someone has to has checked in because the file exists. And then we upload the file. And I when the file is record is into timetec, and then we delete the file. And when the person has the next task, then it will be recorded and will be created a new file. And therefore, we are needing a new palette. And it's called file system.

File System, you have to install it, and then you can access here under Fs access.

And now we want to trigger our, our flow with this axis. Because the first time it has to be checked, if the data, the time record is, is there, therefore we have the path data. And the message file name is a string and it's called time records. dot txt, we read and write it. So let's see if this works. Because now it should be here. And it has two outputs. And when we take here and closer look on the menu, it's the first output means it's accessible. And the second means it's not accessible, or into interesting. So let's see. Here we go. Now, when I'm putting down and chip, we should see an feedback. And we see it's there. And if we delete it, so time records to extend, now it should be gone. It's not here, we're deleting here, then next time, nothing will happen. As you can see I putting you down the chip, but it's not accessible. So let's see. Deploy. Now I'm getting the message because it's on the second output and it's not accessible.

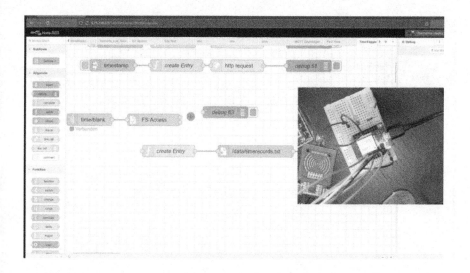

So this is the logic of what we are wanting to have now. So if let me see if the file is not accessible, we are creating the file. If it is accessible, then we want to put out the file. And we could say let's see, we want to have the file. Therefore we have to read the file. And we want to have the the path of it. It's called Data time records TX dear and we want to have fear. There is no chasen available, then we could say he leaving the same bodies was codec Nope. Then I'm adding you and Jason then we are testing the flow right now. So delete everything. Now I'm putting down here, the blank chip. And we're getting here something out. That means now it's created with this one. Let's see. Then I would like to have time records textarea. Perfect. And when I'm now putting the chip a second time. Then we see here on the debug 60 stream. We got here the object perfectly formatted. That's what we want so on then we are not finished yet because we want to set now the auth token. We already did that or not let's not the auth token let's create the entry or what is the best. Let's I would go with the auth token. And now we are not finished yet because we want to manipulate.

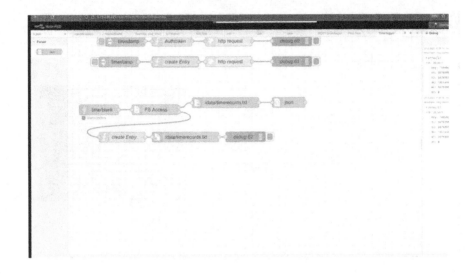

The second entry was the current time therefore we have to make a timestamp with math floor new date. Good time divided by 1000s and we make a new record This is our payload. And this payload of fear, as we can see Cirrus, the object T two is the time. And this will be overwritten with the extra time, because then we know exactly how long the person worked on this specific project. And then we say message dot payload is new records, for example, is the authentification. Header, finish. And then we make your input records and, and Deepak and we have to remove the file, don't forget it. So file system, remove the file, because when it's already on, then we want to delete it so that in the next time, everything works as before. And therefore we want to have the path. And the filename is urine directly in string. And it's called time records dot txt, and then we click on Ah, you will have arrow who can see it, but your debts must be in function. Okay, so let's see if everything works. I'm deleting you the file. So we have the Remove time record okeydoke here, not here, then, let's see, I'm putting now here. Let's switch a little bit to the right. Putting in blank on the error of id Tech, debug 62 that means the record is now on the server perfectly cut time records, it's here, then I would like to work on it. And now let's see TimeTracker delete the last one so that we see if something new comes. Now I'm finished my work, I put in the blank chip once again on and we accepted the array that means we have now entered the record. Let's see if it's on. And here we go we have here from our M Quiddity message, this is what we are transmitting here and we can add here something else. And then this message will be get your into our time taker. And of course we are not really worked along just half of a minute. And also the flow very adding here our time works very well. And is the file now gone. Let's see, it's gone. And perfectly. I'm can also Oops, that was not the right one. I also create here for example, the time ESP chip. Then I deploy it, let's test if it works with the ESP. We have here a new object. And we have accepted it. Let's see if it's also here, absolutely missing. And so our whole example with the terminal with the RFID chips is now finished. And we have also seen here how we can work with flat files. But also you could of course update here the record via the web API. It's also possible but in this case, I would like to show you how you can work with flat files. Because when the server will be restarted and we are logged in, doesn't matter because the file is on this server

# TIME-CONTROLLED PLANT WATERING WITH WATER LEVEL MONITORING WIRING

And as always, we're going through the wiring part at the beginning at the project. So here I'm using the tiny seed studio Chou ESP 32. But of course you can use any other ESP 32 as well, then we have an ultrasonic sensor, which gives us later on the water level or indicates how much water do we have in a in a bottle for example, and then we haven't related because we only want to switch on or off our water pump. And normally, this is used by 12 volts these pumps. So therefore, if you an external power supply and and directly from this power supply, I'm connecting the 12 volt to the downside of this breadboard and the ground will connect it of both sides and the ground will be later on Switched during with the relay.

Here I have one step down converter that means that 12 volts will be converted to five volts for the breadboard and so that we can power up here our ESP and the sensor and as well also the operating voltage for the relay, if the relay switches then the grounds will be yet connected that means the power supply for the water pump is on and then everything will be running as it should be.

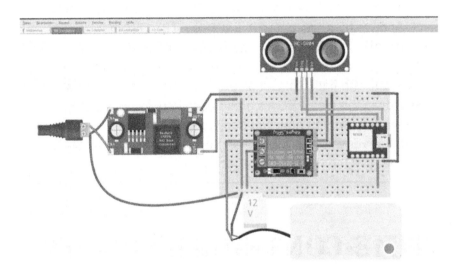

So in my case, I have the USB 32 smaller Russian with this antenna, then I have the ultrasonic sensor so that I can measure here some level with my hand. And I have here this relay, but on the relay there is no water pump because I in the debugging mode, playing around with water is not what I want. So therefore we just hearing later on the clicking from the delay so that we can see if our sketch is working properly. And afterwards. We just can add here, two more delays or three relays, etc. It's always the same also a few of them from the ultrasonic sensors. So we are building up the code so that you can extend this catch. So the because often, when you're creating an automatic watering system, then you're not only using it for a one case and you will use it for many cases, but for the debugging purposes purpose and for learning purpose. We are just having your one cents on and run really.

# FLOW CHART

Let us start in this chapter by going through the flowchart. And here's the finished project. So, that means, what we are going to do is the ESP 32 should send to one of the following M Quiddity topics and message so that these flow will be triggered, then we are fetching data from our Maria DB or MySQL database. And then we can see when was the last time when we wanted our plans, this is why a timestamp made and then we made here and logic which calculators to differentiate the difference between today and the last watering and then we sent a zero on one if the pump should be started or not. If the pump starts then we also get from our router Sonic sensor here the distance and we insert this distance into another table what we also want to do is hear some notification if the water in our container is not or is in a critical level then we can send here for example, adding here and note from telegram or an email node so that we can notify it and in the other case, it's an deep sleep and deep sleep means that we are sending your data to on other tables so that we get know how okay, I was catches working because often we just need only three or four days and watering and therefore, we can check if each hour for example, the USB wakes up and this last one is for the dashboards and to get so no now you get the main idea of what we want to do.

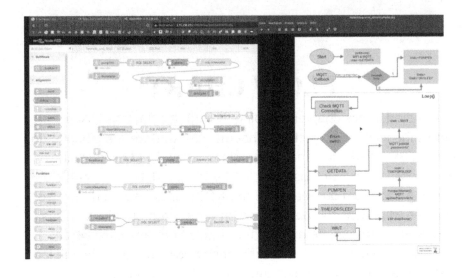

And I would like to introduce you to an basic method what is used when working with microcontroller comes into your mind and this is by using enums enums are an construct where we can save one single state at the time and it helps us because when we are using flags, then we have often the problem should we reset it to bear to be declared etc. So let us go through the main concept. We're starting with the setup we're making the pin molds to Wi Fi and quality data. And we have here an enum and sets the enum of get data. In the loop, we have to check and quality connection. And here are the four states of our enum. This enum has get data pump, time for sleep and weight. And at the first beginning this enum has here gets data so they get data will be started here and then we're sending from the ESP to pump it in for a message. We are have our time logic and then we are sending n one or n zero that you can see and we are here and wait. So the ESP waits, the node read gets the message, the calculation starts and then it sends back on one or zero to pump start. Then the states so this is the callback we are getting here to 01 in the USP. And then we are setting when it's on one we are setting the states to pump or we get to deep sleep. And with this enum we have an comfortable way where we can have our loop in an structured and overview and good overview. And so we are always know in which state we are currently in and then we are now setting up our schedule step by step so that we can create the whole logic as we can see here

# BASIC STRUCTURE WITH ENUMS

We start with our basic sketch. And in this basic sketch, I would like to implement now, the main structure with the enums. So that we have a good starting point. Therefore, I'm jumping to the top. And we are assigned here, a new railroad, it's called enum states. So this will be the blueprint, like we do it in the object orientated way. Now, in other cases, because then it's for me easily easier to identify which variable we are using here. So it's called Get Data, then we have, for example, pumping. Then what else do we had he then with time for sleep, and wait? Time for sleep. And the last one is Wait, no comma at the end. And yeah, I could assign it for example, like this way, states, this is what I made the blueprint. And then I could say, the state, or I could also create another one, it could be handy for other cases, but we only need the first one. So this is just for on training purpose. Then we are uncommenting. This because we are using the short form. And I could write here, right after this one state, this is the same as here. But then you had here both of the variants. So now we are going here into our loop. And we are not using now the current release. But maybe later on, therefore I just commenting out.

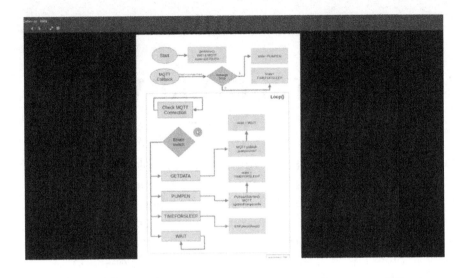

So yeah, I want to make the main loop. So I would like to use here and switch case, because it's pretty easy to read in this case. So what we're doing now, switch. And my variable is now the state because states is the blueprint. And then we're saying case gets data, double points. And this is the first one, what we have here. So let's check again, here is the enum we're starting in the setup, and the first point is state get data. And this is what we want to bring out here. So for examples, your print line gets data I want and quality data. And then we have to do that in the setup. So that means the state should be set to get data. Yes, then we have the very first year, this switch, and then the other cases. So that means we have here our switch, not really finished, because we need a break. Then we have the case pumping, double point, then pump break. Then we copy and paste this one, two more we have then wait. Nothing to do just waiting. And then we have the last one it's going to sleep. So this is called time for sleep and get to sleep. So let's see if I have something misspelled or is everything okay. Looks good to me. So the first test we can make therefore we are uploading the sketch. Don't forget to switch in the platform loan ustedes studio where if you're using or using another platform, another version of this ESP 32 port. And then we are starting here the serial monitor. And now I have no delay, that means I haven't got changed here the credentials. And now we see here, our output. So that means if I'm restarting, we see our M quality connection and Wi Fi connection.

So let's see if it can make you restart. It's too fast, because it jumps directly to the loop. And here we are printing out I want data. And this is now how we can control the main loop because the encoded D callback then later on we are changing the state. And regarding the state of our enum we can make here our functions

# MQTT COMMUNICATION WITH NODE-RED AND ESP32

Now, we are going to the next step that means we want to get here the data. So, that node read will send us actual infos and this will be implemented now, therefore, we are here in our node red we are creating a new flow for example, watering plants and we're adding here and debug and inject and function we need and we are needing here also to encode TT one in and one out. So, these are the basics then the first one is that message from the States. So, get data will send us years some to an topic for example, pump inform So, we are getting your data and this data will then trigger your and flow in our case just for the first purpose we are seeing here and message that payload is data will be sent and or will be created then we sending this data to was that right? Yes it was right then we are sending this data to war Let me see how do we edit for example, start pumps or pump start pump starts serum false then we are connecting the function with this M Quiddity out and of course, I would like to see if there is something going on. And also here I would like to see if there is something Okay, so let's switch here.

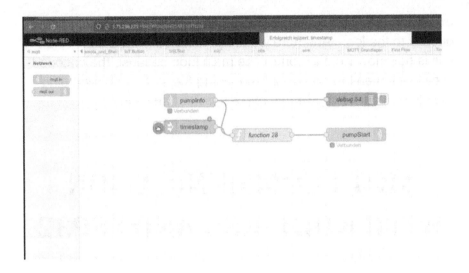

That means I could implement here also an inject to pump start and also yearn to pump info this means this will send from the get state then it triggers this flow what we are creating later and will send us the actual data. Some similar print, I want em Quiddity data, and I would suggest that we are making a new flow a disconnect here so that we don't see your same thing over and over again. Then we're making get data and new functions so that we keep track of our codes jumping to the top. And we could say here White gets data and inside this we make in here and clients dot publish and it's called How do we call it pump info. And we want give me information. Then I also want you and Cyril print line and quantity publish pump in four. Now wait and we'll change the state to wait because we have now sent here and am crudity. So this one sent an MQ DT we are waiting now. And when the callback comes then so we are here in wait when the callback comes. Maybe we are changing to pump or we're going to sleep one of them will be implemented then later on. So this is our waiting scenario and then we switch to Wi Fi em quotidian because we want to implement of course also the callback. But before we can make the callback we have to subscribe to the topic and the topic is called pump start. On this pump starts we want to make an F because Maria here we are getting an Cyril or an one and this will be the main case. And for the first test, we could say here just printing out the message sewer print line and we are saying yeah, I would like to have the message

166

temp. Later on. We make here the if statement. So let's see if the compiler has any errors for us. And while this catches uploading, we are opening yeah that we can see what is going on. So, and we already got the information so attempting M Quiddity collection M Quiddity publish to pump inform now wait message arrived and topic pump start message data will be created and here we only fetched here the data are then the message, the beans our flow works. So the main idea was it just be started to start it getting and tweaking the flow so that we can get the needed information from node right because later on, we want to have here for example some SQL statements and fresh info if we should start the pump or not. And that's what we now implemented

# GLOBALS.H FOR GLOBAL VARIABLES

And now we're preparing the next step. And so that we can use all of these variables also in other files, I would suggest that we are creating here a new file and it's called the Global's dot h. And what we're doing with this Global's is we're defining some variables which are included in all of the other files so that we can have access in other files as well. So therefore, I would say we're making here an includes, and of course, we have to include the Arduino age, and then we're making an include guards with if n def Global's underline H, then define Global's underline H and at the end we're saying, and if so, what we're doing here is this will the compiler checks if such include guards are here. And if I'm now includes the global state H here in the M Quiddity. And in the main, normally, I have done an MRI declaration, if I'm, for example, say, unsigned, a long previous Milly's.

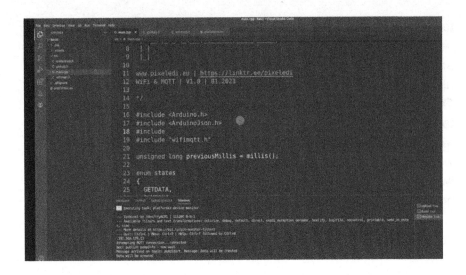

And now I'm implemented here include Global's dot age, and also on the Wi Fi and quotidian. So for example, here, I'm also including the global start age. And if I'm getting rid of these include guards, and then making the checking the compiler, I will have here and redefinition of these variables because I implemented here and that also, I have it here as well. So I'm get rid of that. Once again, let's check here redefinition, because I implemented it here and also in the main and therefore I'm using here some include cards, then with this include cards, the compiler can check isn't already implemented, those Global's dot h and if so, I'm not referencing it anymore. So only one time at at the runtime and as you can see here now there is no problem if I'm implementing here, this is necessary because I want to access here all of the variables and also as well here. So here we have done our global declaration and what I would like to do here is also using these states will copy and paste it into our Global's then what's also from interest is we're creating the variable for their relay and it's called my my blend is called pump look straight down this is the name of my plant and some pin 20 And it's called and const by it and for the age for the ultrasonic sensor we are using here two pins it's the first pin is the trigger one and we have a short one. So you can add easily other HR sensor as well and we are using later on and function where you can easily access a few of them. Then we of course need also year and distance one and you can have here and distance two as well. Because here we are later saving the distance from the sensor till the surface of our water so that we know exactly how much water is in it.

# CREATE MARIADB TABLE AND USE DATABASE NODE

Now we want to create the databases with AD minor and we are already used at minor was to port 8080. And you have comes to ServerName, from Maria dBm and our credentials and with the right credentials. And now we can either create a new database, and the name of the database could be for example plants. database has been created, and then we can create some tables. The first table could be we could call it deep sleep blends. And what we want to do here is that we get each time the ESP 32 goes to deep sleep that we get here and timestamp. And this is all what we want to have. So it's, we, of course, we use your 24 multiplies 356 in the year that means roughly 9000 entries in a year, this is absolutely okay. It doesn't need too much space. And therefore I have always the opportunity to see if the sketch works right or not.

Then we click on save and we've created our first first table. Next table. That could be for example, we could say blends, level or watering level as they would like I'm putting in an idea without the increment. And in the next field we are seeing and timestamp and we could in the search row for example, level one or distance one I think it's called distance one, we can also add the edit distance to one and click on Save. And now we created the two tables which we can later use in the node read. So let's test if if we have you in connection so we already installed here the MySQL node then double click on it. We want to have the IP address the port root the database is now blends. Then we click here on finished. Just see if we can get here the connection to our database and here we go. We have here and green sign that means no rights can access our just created databases and tables.

# STORE WATER LEVEL INFORMATION IN MARIADB

And now we want to create the SQL statements so that we can insert the the distance level from our watering. Therefore, I need here a new function nodes and we are connecting, so heal them flow will be triggered with the color with the water this dense, then we are connecting here, Maria DB nodes. And of course, we can also have here NP back and this SQL statement looks now the following. So first we take a closer look at what we want to have here, we have and timestamp distance one and distance two Versa could use here floats for example, I've added the integer and yes, timestamp distance one distance two.

So, let's current timestamp is math because I would like to create the timestamp here in Node red and not in the database gets time. And we remember we want the seconds and not the milliseconds therefore we divided 2000 Yeah, and then we say for example, it's called distance one. Distance one is message payload, this distance one. So we are accessing now the object which we are get referenced, then in this variable, the number 16 is saved. Then we have your distance tool. And now we could make our SQL statements topic. And it's called insert into the table name, the table name is plants level. Then we need so it's called timestamp. Distance one, distance to values and the values we have here. First of all the timestamp. And we'll have to break up here the string because this is now an end, very urban. Then comma plus plus distance one and we have the distance to saw. And we're returning this message so that the SQL statement will be taking into consideration for the note. Then, once again here I'm holding the hand before the sensor I manually trigger the sensor. So let's see. A new object will be arrived. We getting in Okay. Then let's see a select data. And there we go. We have here and new distance five and 22 Is this right? We can't see der so let's check here five is okay. And the Unix timestamp. We also conference can convert it convert. And now it's March 23 914. Exactly what we have now. Perfect. So our whole sketch is working well. Once again, I'm testing it. We're getting the second object back, select data. And there we go. We have the eight and we also have media. The next step in our project that we could save your data from node read directly to Maria DB

# MONITOR WATER TANK LEVEL

Now we want to create an logic, where we can see if the water goes nearly to the end in our container. And therefore, we are triggering it manually at the first beginning, then we want to have here Esquel select. Then of course, we need here in my squirrel nodes. And then and logic where we calculate the difference. And then we want to have yet and debug for the first test. So the SQL statement could be select distance one from blends level, order by IDM. DSC limit one looks great to me. And now in this function, we want to calculate how much water do we have left, so therefore, we set let distance one is message that payload, sips zero and it's called distance one, then we would like to have an container size.

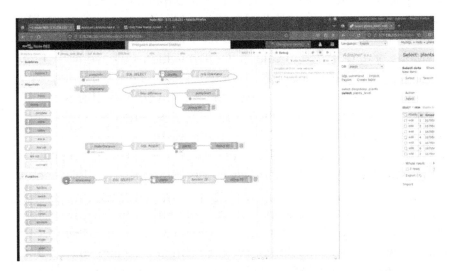

So for example, it's 24 centimeters high, and then we have 1/3 of it is for example 16. So let's test it out. If we can get here the right

values then trigger this flow we getting here back on 28 here the function 20 And and what do we get em also an array with distance 20 And is this right? Let's see Select Data 20 is the last one perfect okay, then we can go further on and could say here. If the distance one is greater or equal 1/3, then we should be notified on edits Nothing should happen. That means we could now for example, set an email node and telegram notification or whatever you want. And then you get for example, because he in the calculation, you can see then, aha, the water level isn't a critical dimension, I have to water the container again. So that pumps not get trying and this could be done here in this flow.

# DEEPSLEEP TO SAVE POWER

And now, we want to add also our deep sleep function, but before we do that, we can add the current flow also to the main floor. And we can do that for example with some links. So we could say for example here is in zinc out, that means, for example, when I would like to add the end delay, when the water level is insert, then after two seconds I would like to have here and link out, double click on link out it's called after what distance save in dBm. And now, I can add here and link in and this link in goes to the Esquel select and this is called Check water level and notification then we are linking this with the watering plants. And as you can see here, if I'm not clicking on the link, then we have here and good overview so I can manually trigger this flow to check if it should be I have to deploy it, I can manually check if there is something happened and of course, you could add here the telecom LSVT it in the other example or an email note, and when we are inserting the insert the water distance also after two seconds, these flow will be triggered. So um, but we are not finished yet. Because now we want to add here the deep sleep in our flow because you're in the loop time for deep sleep nothing happened so far. And therefore, I would like to print out a Serial print line I am going to sleep then I would like to client publish records. Deep Sleep doesn't matter what we are inserted here. So publish. Because this is also not implemented yet switching back here to one to node red. And we are ones now and M Quiddity here and m Quiddity. In then we want an SQL insert. We want plants. And I would like to have fun Deepak.

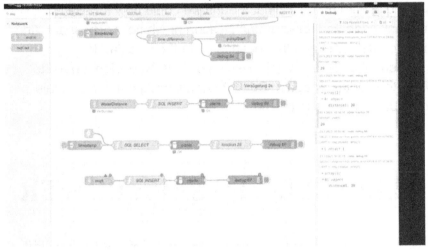

So now this was called record deepsleep. SeRa. And then we could say, well, you need to timestamp. Of course you can use also the timestamp in the database as well. So let me see what do we have here. Deep Sleep plans into deep sleep plans, just a timestamp. We'll use just a current timestamp. So we could use nearly all of the same from here. Let me see I need the brackets looking good so far. Then we click on the deploy. And this is now in production. And now we have add here something for our deep sleep and I would add the end delay. And then we go to deep sleep. This is a configuration for the ESP 32 from seed studio. And then afterwards, normally, we could change the get data here. But this will never be really get into productive because afterwards when the deep sleep is finished. We have to of course also adhere to deep sleep for example here. That means one hour because it's microseconds, then the USB starts all over again. So this is just for security issues that we are not keeping into an endless loop. And I'm deactivating the use of deep sleep because in the debugging mode it's not very useful because then always the the was beyond device is not recognized, and therefore we're just making en delay from five seconds, or I would say for 10 seconds.

```
 88        getData();
 89        break;
 90    case PUMPING:
 91        startPumping();
 92        break;
 93    case WAIT:
 94        // nothing to do just waiting
 95        break;
 96    case TIMEFORSLEEP:
 97        // get to sleep
 98        Serial.println("I am going to sleep ZzzZZzZZZZzZZ");
 99        client.publish("recorddeepsleep", "zzZZzzZZ");
100        delay(1000);
101        esp_sleep_pd_config(ESP_PD_DOMAIN_RTC_PERIPH, ESP_PD_OPTION_OFF);
102        //ESP.deep void delay(uint32_t)
103        delay(5000)
104        state = GETDATA;
105        break;
```

And then we switching to get data so we can test if our sketch is working properly. And also if we are filling in here, some records for the deep sleep, checking if everything is right, and then the first entry is already made. So we got also an zero because we have what is our time difference now 30 seconds, so also the second one isn't zero because we have a delay for 10 seconds. So two of them weren't active, the next one should be delivered on one because yes, the logic is functioning. So that means we are saving you two data's we will getting back one data selected. Here we go. Because also when it's not pumping, I'm getting in record for the deep sleep as you can see, and zero. So I can always check if the current sketch is working properly. If there is any problem here, I can see how there is too much time delay, and I have to check my ESP. So tune zeros. The next one should give me a new value. Yes, it's pumping all over again. Let's see deep sleep plans select data and here we have the new one. So once again, I would like to check it so I should have Now getting back and serum the first serum now the USB is in deep sleep then I should get here and second zero, there we go on the second deepsleep should also be entered. And now this is the actual data. Now the last one yes, let me check. If we get a new data. Here we go. We get the new data and also the

175

deep sleep plans is working correctly. So 10 is the last one now I should have 11 That's it what we want

# VISUALIZATION OF DATA ON DASHBOARD

Now the workflow is nearly finished, if you would like you can visualize it also with a dashboard. Therefore, I need here and we control something that I can inject manually, I need an SQL Select, and MySQL node and function nodes. And I would like to have here some UI elements, the first element could be let me see and chart. And I would like different texts, the text could be let me see here, we're starting right again, with Mr. SELECT statement at the very first beginning. So the Select could be a message topic, select from blends level, and I would like to have the last one, then we will get it then to the function nodes. And now let's see what we can do with this function node. I would like to have here two or three outputs. Therefore I go to setup click on three outputs. And now in the function, we are creating here, three message objects. And we could say, let container size is 24 that we need later on for the visualization. And now the first one is message zero dot payload, is the size of it from the container minus message payload. And we are getting back on one entry for one tupple from the database. And it's called distance one, we also can use this variant not only with the brackets, message zero or topic, how is it called, for example, in my case, it's called clicks VEDA, we use them later on for visualization, then the message one for the second client, we only have one place hold on, then I would like to see when the last time we get watered the plants because often you only need oil every three days or each day. And therefore, it's good that we have here and date object is new date, message payload. And it's called the timestamp.

```
1  let msg0 = {};
2  let msg1 = {};
3  let msg2 = {};
4
5  let container = 24;
6
7  msg0.payload=(container - msg.payload[0].distance1);
8  msg0.topic="Glücksfeder";
9
10 //msg1 for the second plant
11
12 let dateObject = new Date(msg.payload[0].ti
13
14 return msg;
```

And we have to multiply the timestamp with 1000 because JavaScript uses milliseconds. Then we have to format everything. And we could say var or let human date format is date object. And we could say to local date string. And I would like to have here the German ones. And now as a last point message to payloads is the human date format. And the message to topic is last watering. So and now we returning all of the three objects or objects. The first one is the message zero message one message two. That means at the first output, this container or this entry will be delivered and the second one nothing because it's just a placeholder. And then the last one the message tune. So there we go. Then we could he for example, if the chart and hear the text, and then we could edit the chart as well. Therefore, we have to add here a new group and also a new top I would go another way. Let's go another way. First of all, we click on the right side onto the dashboard. And we create a new tab. And this tab is now called we click on edit and this tab is called watering plants. Here we could add here of course also an icon and that's good. Then we can use your our chart and we say for We're example, where is it? We need a new group as well into the top of watering plants. And now we have here the size, the size should be all over the size. Then we have here, the child's name, it's called watering levels, I would like to have here and this kind of diagram, we say the minimum is zero, the maximum is 24. This is the size of my of the container, then I would like to have this column. Yeah, I think this sounds very good to me. Finished. Then the next one, we have to change it also the group the group is watering plants. The size is outdoor, the text is last watering. And here the value now is message payload. In the distant ducks, yeah, we'll click on Finish. Let's see what the EU will looks like. Dashboards, then we have here watering plants. And then we see here nothing because maybe we have here, enter something let's see. Then let's check if we have here some mistake in the ship. In the function 29. Maybe here the payload is not correct. So let's test it with synthetic well, you finish, deploy and then let's insert here something but nothing is shown here.

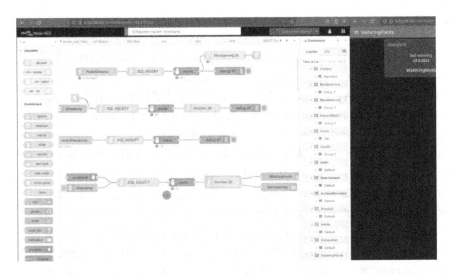

So the problem was, we have to change the size manually not in the case of automatic. So for example, six by four finish. And now we are getting here, the last watering and also the watering level. So I can jump back here. No steady Quilliam, recalculating it, then we restarting it. And there we go, this is our last value on the UI control can be linked for example, to one of the previously flows and then when we add in here and a new value also, let's see. Let's plug and play here. The ESP 32. Watering is now on let's see the debug note that we get the new debug and distance much to higher. What's going on here, I have to hold the hand before because we that's not possible in this case. And now we have seven. And we can see here that we have here a lot of water because seven is just the level from the top to the water and that means we have 24 sides of the container therefore we have enough water in it. Great visitors realisation and now we have the perfect automated water plants for us including also a notification when something goes wrong or when something when the water is in a critical level.

# FLASHING TASMOTA

Starting in this chapter by discussing what is this motor and why we should use it. So, normally, when we are buying such smart plugs there is an ESP chip insight or often or also other frequencies like CPM but in this course we are focusing on the Wi Fi connection, and therefore an ESP chip, it could be an 8266 or an other smaller version, but often it's with less chibios Because we don't need so much GPS insights and smart clock and therefore, the Wi Fi connection is still there.

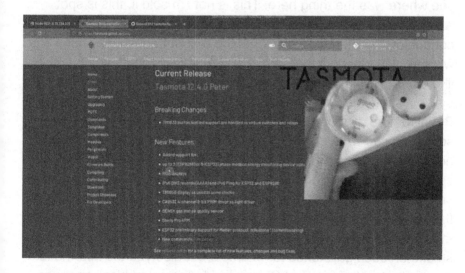

And then we can flesh here this motor and what is this motor. This motor is an open source firmware for ESP devices and we can control the M quality wire and weaponry but also can use here HTTP for example, s and s and service. And that's what we want to have we want to control our smart plugs as we have here in uncomfortable way and in open source so that we not using any third party apps like the this one from corazones. That's the reason why I think does Moto is such a great opportunity. So therefore, I would like to show you on the smaller side on GitHub, you can click on supported devices. And here you can see for example by supported modules, what you can use, which sockets you can use, but be aware a lot of them are hardware act. And what do I mean with hardware HECT I feed it goes on the ESP and there is exactly shown what they did. So that means they cracked up the whole house thing so that he can get inside the smart block. Then they cut down and productive conductor. It's really not a good idea. And then you can get inside the smart block and can wire you out so let me see here is the ESP 8285. And then where it sits. Here we go. Here's the chip and then you can flash it why you out with an FTDI controller. And then within tasmota Eisah you can flash here tasmota on it but once again that's not the preferred way because you are here opening and smart block which yeah has a lot of power in it. And the problem is and that's really a problem so let me see where was the thing here. This is not I'm sold it, this is spot welded. And normally you have not the right tools to spot welds the conductor and therefore this is not the recommended way but if you want to, you can do it there are also other kinds of let me see others like here just with some just with some screws and then you get inside it's much easier to hardware hack those plugs for example. But also here, when you take a closer look like here I was to go sons, you can write goes on directly. And then with the app, you need to send them a few information and then it's possible that they send you an update for the for your smart plugs and then it's not too smart on it but then you have here and version which can be flashed over the air. And with a little Google research you can find then later on. Also good examples how you can flesh over the air to smoke on such gallstones for example but also you the information for you. asked before what Chip is inside the smart block because not every goes on for example has an ESP inside the also the always switching of regarding the supply chain, different kinds of chips and when there is no ESP chip inside then you can't use here in this way Deus moto.

# CONFIGURE TASMOTA

So I assume you have already flashed the device, and also configured so far that you can access it. And when you can exit it like here, and as you can see, I can now toggle it via the web UI here. It goes on goes off. And what I would like to do now is to show you what you what we can do that will make the right configuration so that we can later use also M qu TT. And when we go to the console, we have here different views on it. And I would like to go through a few. So that was the first one. So that we can see what options do we have? First of all, we should set here the voltage and that could be done by wattage set. And it depends on which regions are you live. Here we have a voltage from 213 in AC and AC voltage, then up console and the command and now we are setting the voltage to 230. Then as the next one we could set here at the TD periods. That is how often do I get here and update. And this is in seconds. So for example, I could say I would like to have here every 20 seconds, or let's just test it every five seconds, I would like to have that tasmota sends me here and the actual data all of them what is captured.

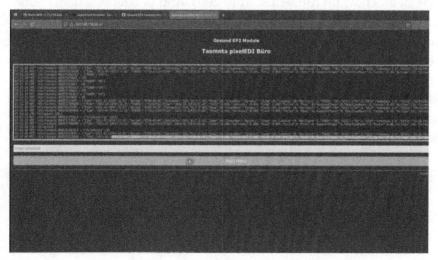

So let's see. If it works, we can see here the state and the sensor. Yes, it works. So but not five seconds is a little bit too much. So let's say 20 seconds, for now. Then also we can switch on and off via the black. So when I'm now entering power on then it's of course it was already on then let's see power off. Now it's off. And those are information which we will need later on in Node rates. That's also the reason why we do that. So now I'm turned it off with power on, we can turn it on via their console. Also, we can set an IP address here, I have already set it to 68. And when I'm entering now I haven't static IP address. Then also relevant is the timezone. In my case, it's the timezone 99, you can get all of this information from tasmota. Here on the commands examples, you see all of the examples, which we already use to run time soon. Then what's also interesting is here, power on state. So let's search it what do we have what options we have power on state control the power state when the device is powered up? And that's interesting, because maybe when there is when you plug it in or when there is some voltage cut etcetera, what is the behavior what you would like to have, and I would like to have it on one because when I plug it in, it should be turned on. But maybe you have your something that should keep turned off. But normally on frigerator he would always like to have it on and he you have the possibilities then the LED status is also something what I would like to change here. So take a look at this now on ISIL led start to zero. And of course it takes your power because in a normal way. In a normal production environment. You don't need an LED because it's somewhere behind the furniture and therefore you can see it but here in our debugging state. I keep it on and Lady state one. Yes, it's on. Okay. And now we are ready to go. So go to our main menu. And now we have calibrated and set up data smarter so that we can do in the next step the equity connection.

# SWITCHING TASMOTA SOCKETS WITH NODE-RED

Now we want to switch the test mode with no dread. And therefore, we are going back to our main menu from the small town. And we are going to click on Configuration and configure MQ dt. And therefore we are inserting our hosts without the without the HTTP. And then we are connecting the port 1883. We are putting in our username and the password. And be aware click here on this small checkbox. And of course, you can change here some prefixes etc. But I'll leave everything the same here and these three input fields and click on safe, then does motor configuration is saved device will restart in a few minutes. And I think that's it. And you can see I've plugged in here and charging device from a smartphone so that I see here, a few values. And now we can check if there is something sent to us.

And we can use here the illiquidity Explorer, and I'm connecting directly to the, to the broker. And now we can see here, every connection, what is made, you can see and surely, but this is for later purposes, he's also some Taylor thing. Ah, and here we have into small time. Let's see em, that's interesting. So then I would like to change here, the console, and you're changing the TD period to five seconds, always was 10 is the minimum. And now we should see each 10 Second, the actual date. And when I click on it, you can see here, what we get here, the actual current periods, the total start time, everything what we want, are here updated. And as you can see here, when there is a new a new values transmitted, let's see now, and we also have a T and M quality explorer, to see how we can access it. And here we have to tailor topic, and then it comes to this motor, this is the name from it. And here we have the center, or this date, both of them are possible endpoints for us. And this is what we now want to do, and the note rates. So therefore, we need here to inject and one n quantity out. Then I would like to have the n string with on and then string with off and asked the question, how could we assign now the topic. So let's put both Windows besides. And, you know, we did it before power off for example. And now we can see here ah, that's the command what I would like to have, but I'm not using you the stat I'm using here the CM, N D command CMD for command. And then I'm using the editor smarter. Nope, that was the first. Not that doesn't work. Once again to smooth. Right click Copy and and as the last one power. So let's try it out. If this works, finish, then connect those two to the topic. Because this we're sending in, on and off as we do it also here in the command line. So when I'm clicking here, power on, it goes on. And when I'm clicking here, you're now on off. Let's see. Now it's on, we got the on, we're clicking on off, and it's off. Once again. You can see here and Lydia and now we are clicking off and we're clicking on perfectly. That's is what we want to achieve. Now with the node read interface. We're sending an on and off to our tasmota and this is the right topic. And with the command we can send the wire M Quiddity. Also our test motor commands.

# READ SENSOR DATA FROM SMART PLUG

Now we want to have the data what we have from the console also here in our node reds therefore needing an equity in and not an out and we also need again Deepak There we go, we connect both of them and what we want to have here is exactly those topic and we are seeing and sensor data is that what we want with Taylor. So let's copy this one double click Change the topic name, qu s on serum full screen then, here we go. And we are setting the tiller period of 10 I think was the minimum and there we go. Here we have our overview we have here the total amount then we see what we needed today.

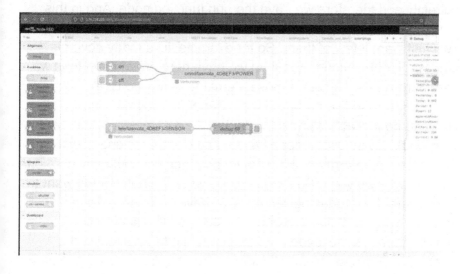

And we getting the actual data on it. That's exactly what we want. So let's click on the main menu, we see the date we see the energy arrested today kilowatt hours in my case, then with the voltage the actual current Yes, with that case, we can also have a lot of information and also can visualize and also can make here the proper for example, monitoring when for example here the energy gets to uncertain level then we can send us some informations etc.

# SAVE ENERGY DATA IN INFLUXDB AND VISUALIZE IN GRAFANA

Now we want to save the data into influx dB. And this is an easy one for us, because we already know how to do that. Therefore, we need one more function, because we can't directly save it into influx dB, then we are needing an influx, the B note in flux dB. recollecting those, the settings will be in that the influx DB B, that's okay. And organization, the bucket is an old read. And organization is pixel ID in this case. And what we also want to have here, for example, a new measurement has motor. And now we can send the values directly and therefore we have the and function node. And in this function node we are grab those values, what we have here, and we just want a few of them. So for example, let's today power is message dot payload. And then we have here energy and then we are here we can access it those elements. And I would like to have here today. And I've prepared the other ones. So here we are, have voltage power, active and total. And now we're making urine and payloads. So message dot payload, and we are making now those variances is an array and the object and then we could say here our words what we want. So for example, we take whatever we want to write here, then today power, then we have here the voltage power, etc, are prepared also this one saw, then, so it looks prettier. That's it will return this message. And that should it be let's test it. If it works, how can we check it? Nope, here I have the wrong influx dB. Once again, looking good, then we are switching to our influx db to the datasource. To the packet node read we have the measurement tasmota.

That's the area. And here are our values. And those values are how we defined it in the function. So when you would like to have your other words, then use it other keys submit. There we go you we have our values. And those values we can perfectly visualize in Grafana. Therefore we go on because we are ready set up here the data's communication. And we could now set up your new dashboards. For example, new panel. And as we did before, I would like to have your descriptive copy the script pasted in. But be aware and think that this should be the correct data source. I have a few of them. So let's see. I would like to have here. The Yeah, the active power would be nice. The rest of it we are deleting for the first part, or no the word that would be also nice. Is the voltage here let's see. wattage because with the wattage, we can also do something and so then let's see. That's the well use looking good so far. But I would like to have NASM Gulch for example. And here we could say the maximum is 240 for example, and the value standard value on voltage is the wattage safe. There we go. We have our voltage panel title, world church. And then we could say yeah, adding a new panel, new panel, pasting in the criteria and we have the active power that's also what we want to have. But now in in Time Series power and Let's have it here a little bit more with opacity opacity and around you can also use bars if you would like, but only the point is, I think too, not too big. So, gradient modes units, you can also use some units but I would like to have just yeah we can visualize it here, setting up here the voltage. Now we could say here the last 30 minutes, and it should be each 10 seconds, automatically updated. And with the cycle a few modes with here and really nice dashboard, where we can overwhelm obviously overview our main power consumption and as you can see here, it's absolutely correct in in time, so what do we have here active power 1516 What is no 16 volt amperes apparent power? Very, very good. And of course, of course the energy today would also be interesting. So that we can calculate also multiplies with our currently electricity costs, then we know exactly how much power we have consumed.

# SHELLY 1PM SETUP

I would like to talk with you about the Shelly 1pm. And this is really a great device because you can see it's an power metering relay, and switch with 16 amperes. Because the other smart block which we had, which we had with tasmota, only could toggle 10 amperes. And we can use it with Bluetooth and also with Wi Fi. And as you can see, it's really small device, you can use it behind flush mounted socket, for example. And this is what I did I have someone in my office, it's the first socket, and normally all the sockets are connected in zero. So when I'm using this between the first socket, I can switch off all of my sockets from the office with this relay and other use cases, as we have it here. With an light bulb for example, you can also connect it directly to this light bulb. And you can also use here and contact it's called SW and with this contact you can connect here and normal switch so you have the possibility to switch it with the normal switch and via the web interface for example, with this Shelly and is surely has also an ESP on it, you can also flesh the Shelleys with and smarter but I don't recommend it because the Shelly devices are really great or the Shelly configuration.

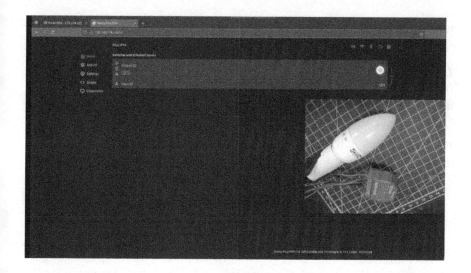

So let's see your firstly when you have connect the shelleyan You found it in your Wi Fi connection. And in the first setup, you go to Settings, then you click on Wi Fi and connecting to your normal router so that we have access it in the same network that's much more comfortable. Be aware that we should configure on the access points. This is the access point you can also enable it or disable it but it would be nice if we can execute it directly with the web server on the ESP when we we are Meteor some some mistakes but therefore I recommend to use some password protection because otherwise everyone in the near can see that you're using and surely I can connect to it. Here I'm keeping this off because we ended Deepak face, he will find all of your you can find all of your Wi Fi settings also Bluetooth. and here also some other settings. The first thing what we will do is now go on settings. And we want to add the firmware and make checking for on new firmware. I'm using the latest one so this is okay. And now we can switch already our Shelly black with the web interface and when we are clicking on you can see here the power consumption the voltage and the actual current. And here we have other things like schedules etc really, really nice. When you click on settings, we also have here the M Quiddity settings. And of course we can add here also all of the things what we want to do. So enable encoded a protocol yes enable RPC aware M Quiddity. Yes, but those two things we're not taking on because this will be sending automatically status information to include it here. But we want to trigger them by ourself. We could change something if we would like type in our username and password for em Quiddity broker and tip from the broker, click on save settings and then you getting an directly feedback if it's connected or not. So let's check it. Save Settings save successful and we can also see if we are connected or not. And this is the first settings what we want to do so that we can later on X is added by a node right

# SHELLY AND NODE-RED VIA RPC

All of this surely devices have good API documentation. And we have to distinguish between the generation one and the generation to the generation one was really easy via HTTP requests, to acquire and also to, to control. Nowadays, we have two generation two devices. And the generation two devices has a completely different approach when it comes to the API. So therefore, I go to devices, I officially plus 1pm. And here I have all of the things what I can do with these kinds of Shelleys. But nevertheless, if you haven't yet another shaly, it's nearly the same approach, but a little bit different in the settings. So what I would like to do now is that we click here on MQ TTM. And that you can see a year a few informations because the first thing what we would like to do is to getting information from the shellye, really, via the API. And here we can see what we can do here, we can get the status, the configuration, etc, all of the things we can access. And then for example, here to get status. So is there an example also in it, let me see. Here we gone. For example, you can post it with like and chastened format like this. And we're getting back then, yeah, our configure raishin. But the main thing is that the whole communication with the Shelleys are now working with RPC. So let's see if we find here something RPC, RPC channels, and RPC protocol.

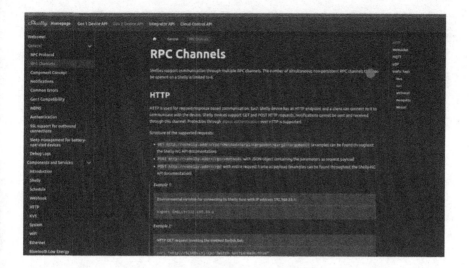

So Shelley supports communication through multiple RPC channels, the number of simultaneous EDI nonpersistent RPC channels that can be opened on a Shelly is limited to six. And the protocol means that or Shelley RPC means remote procedure calls the system RPC. And this is also what we are using now, when we are here in the node red. So let's switch here to node red, then we're making this window a little bit smaller switching back here to the M Quiddity status, because this is the first thing what we want to acquire. So that you get here and good overview of what we want to do. Therefore, we trigger our flow then we need the and function and we need the n m qu TT out and one M Quiddity in and of course, n Deepak. So there we go, connecting every node together. And the main workflow is now we are triggering the flow we have here and function which gives us for example, and add get status. I would like to have the status from the shell here. And I would like to communicate not via request, I would like to have the wire the RPC. So I'm switching here to curl and this parameter or this parameter, I have to post through the RPC channel to get something back.

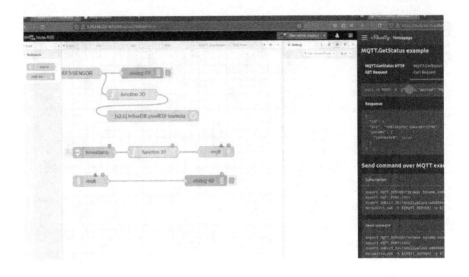

And what I can do now is, I'm using this function and then name it M Quiddity. Get status. And, oops. Then we want to have here some idea. For example, we can make here also and random idea, random idea is math floor, math, random. And we have here and random ID. And then we could say let's new message. And the new message will also be returned. Don't forget that the new message dot payload have now all of this information, which we need here. So the first point is your an ID. Therefore, we saying yeah, that was not right. The idea, double point, random ID, comma, then the source is node read info and I come to it later what I mean with that node read info. Then the next one is the method. And the method is now what we want to acquire what should be the function and this is called the M qu DT Yeah, dot get status. And this is my payload. So I've created this payload. But I edit here the source because I want to have the callback here on Node red info. And I have to send the RPC status to Shelly plus 1pm slash RPC. How do I get to this? Really simple, because let me see here under Settings and could idiom use the encoded the prefix. And this is what I did here. It's the Shelly plus 1pm. And slash RPC is open for any kind of informations or for the APC channel. And once again, here I gave in to the source, the source is now the node read info node read info, is my topic. But with RPC, don't forget it. RPC also is needed here. And all of the information which I want now to acquire will be sent here to this one. So let's test it. I sent now these information out and getting back to the node read info RPC. You can see it here on this one, the idea and your connection is true. So let's acquire more things. So for example, I would like to have another timestamp and not a function. And we're connecting these two the same output. But now I would like to have here, let's go back. Let's go back to my device, for example system. And I would like to have the system get status. Let's see it nearly the same. So that means I have been random idea. And the source is the same. Because I want like to have the same callback, and it's now called sis, get status finished Deployer. Let's see what we get here. And here, we get seen back, the result, restart is false, we get the actual time from the shelleyan. Then we see the RAM size, everything what are available updates. As you can see here, a lot of information, we can go further, let's go back this just for testing all of the the RPC channels so that you get to know what we can do here. And we I would like to go here also on switch, here we go because this is what we are using later on. And also from the switch, I would like to get the status, click concur. Here, we have a lot of information as well. Then we copy those two are also connected here. With this surely RPC button. Now, this is not the get status, this is the status. And now we have the switch status. So the switch status, as we can see here has more things in its source, which git status, but afterwards, we have here and nested objects, so it's called params. And this params has next object, and here we have an idea. And with this ID we're sending in zero. So let's see if this works. And we're getting back the information from the switch itself, we can see here, all of the voltage, the power, what we are just using. So I'm switching on now the light so that we can see that now the light is on. And I want to have the information now from the status. Turning off, and now we can see here, that's the actual voltage. That's the a power and current wellness. Very good. And this is also the thing what we're using later on, but you can see we can have here, one RPC channel with different kinds of chases what we're sending out and getting a different information back and all of this will be sent back to our main In node red InfoSource which we are declared here in the function notes

# TOGGLE SHELLY WITH NODE-RED

And of course, we also can switch on and off our shellye device with Node red. Therefore, we jumping back to the main overview of the shell plus 1pm. I would like to have to see what the switch can do. And we want to have the switch set switch sets, the method sets the output of the switch component to on or off, it can be used to trigger web hooks, as well. So we have an idea, we have an Boolean, true for switch on false otherwise, this is required. And optional. Also here flip back timer in seconds. Interesting. So we can switch it on. And after a few seconds, we can switch it off as well. So therefore, I would like to have here another timestamp.

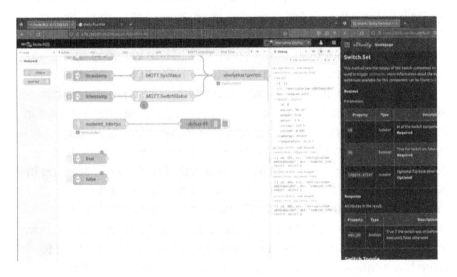

This one will be what do we have here? True or false? So we could feel Boolean true. Then we have here and Boolean false. Then let's copy. Yeah, those one. So with n switch dot set, we leave the random number. But you also can add here and static number. So this is called now switch set as method. The node read info is the same method switch set. Not and now at the end, we have to add here also something and it's called your params. Because these are the params what we want to have params. Double point. And now the information, what we have here, so an idea. Serum. Then we have here and on. And we have here an on off. So let's do here and variable. And this variable we are fetching here. Let on off is message dot payload from before. I think this looks good. So let's see if I forget something No. Then let's test it. Then we're connecting those two together. And we also want the and debug or no debug we want to have here the output of the surely one RPC em, we also can connect it directly but gives us a better view. Okay, then let's test it. Yes, but you can see anything. Then we click on true. It goes on false. True, False. Nicely. What do we get back here we're getting back an object. So let's see what is the result through was on Okay, I see also what was the last you can see it What was the last result it was before on false and now it's an on and this is it what we can do here. And also let's draw off this toggle after.

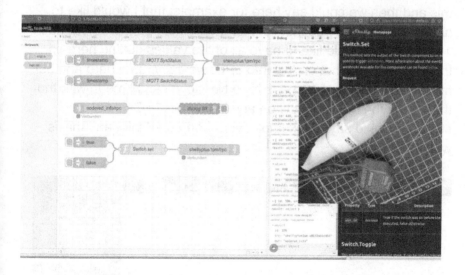

So I've added here at the very end here and toggle after. And let's see what we get in here. Arm toggle after three finish. That means I'm turning now on their conceit once again, it's now in true and after three seconds it will be turned off automatically and this is the toggle after point what we had here. So it's also interesting. So this is from another example Don't worry. And here this toggle after will be used here. For example if you want to automatically switch these back

# RELAY TEMPERATURE MONITORING WITH TELEGRAM NOTIFICATION

And now we would like to simulate that we are monitoring a few values and if one value is too high for example, then we would like to get your an email or on telegram notification, etcetera. So, therefore, we using here and next timestamp, then I would like to have to switch status and also and surely plus one RPC and that I not have to manually invoke here those flows, we could combine this and then we could say here for example, that I would like to have your each 10 seconds just for the training purpose now, each 10 seconds, I would like to have all of the values getting here on this info LPC, but not on this info LPC, we can create here another m Quiddity in so that we have here two flows. And I mean with that, that this is the memory flow on and inside this M Quiddity get started, I would say for example, your node read info, and this is with the interval.

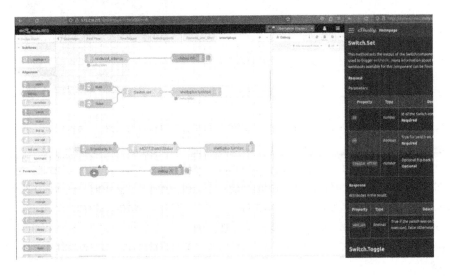

Double click finished, then here is the RPC sera finish deploying, and now I'm getting here each 10 seconds or every 10 seconds, I get the new information from my Shelly 1pm to this topic, as you can see here, and Deepak 17. And here, I can manually get the status from this, this is also an convenient behavior and that you here, edit the source and then you get an A different kind of M Quiddity in your values. So what we can do now is we can process this data, because for example, I would like to have here on this in we can add here and function nodes. And we can process these data and for example, I would like to monitor here, the temperature in Celsius, because in when it's in somewhere mounted in flush mounted aways, maybe the temperature is increasing. So therefore, we are simulating here, the value of monitoring. And therefore, for example, we could say here, double click temperature. Of course, you can also observe here and other projects as well, then lead new message is in your object.

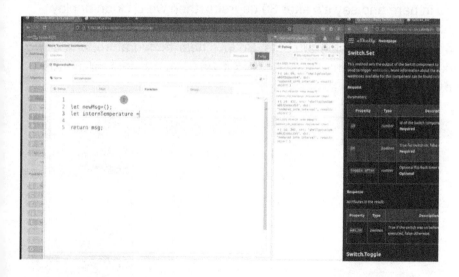

And we could say let's intern temperature is message payloads then we have here I think it's called result result object then we have here the temperature and besides the temperature it's called TCM can see we have the axis here all of these key parameters, then we have the temperature and then we could say for example, if the intern temperature is greater than 60 degrees Celsius, then new message dot payload will make a new brand new object then we copy this and here we are adding for example to check it because I would like to have two minute read bots. We already used it and telegram bots, these are from the last examples of your photos and I would like to have done getting here and message if for example, this is the temperature is too high. Therefore my check ID I already have then we have fear and message content I already prepared it for example, surely temperature is to hire and we also can add here the temperature in turn temperature and we also have the payload it's called temperature and I it's called message okay and what do we need we need a topic and it's called shellye values for example. Then we return of course the new message but not always just in case if this is too high. So and therefore we also need Indian telecom sender There we go. Then we have added the telegram to on Node red call spot. Pam. Then we click on deploy. Looking good so far, but with not getting any thing because we have set it to 60 degrees or 60 degrees. And I'm not heating up the shelleyan. We go in here and say it's after 30 degrees, then we click on deploy. And then in the next three or 10 seconds, we should get the N message in our telegram bots. So let's hear temperature, aha or we have here, problem. So let's check if we have the right temperature. If node one intern temperature.

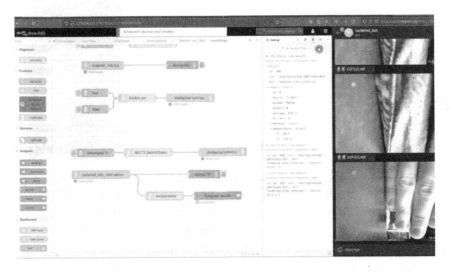

Let's see if we have it right. undefined. Aha, there we go. So it's called result, then it's called temperature. And then we have I have a small there we go, we should have here. So let's check again. If there is a message coming, now, we should get here. There we go. Then we can do this no drawn away because we don't need it anymore. Once again, deployed. And here we got, surely temperature is too high, 49.4 degree, is it right? Great. There we go. And of course, you can use it also. So to edit this, because I'm not getting spammed now. And you can use of course, these logic for other values as well. For example, if it's too high, if the voltage is too high, if it's has to spend too much energy of the day, you have here the AE energy in the total. And also from the last few minutes, because I haven't got it turned on. So now it's on. So let's see if there is some other values now. And now we should have here some energy also in total. And in the last minute in the last second, two minutes, last three minutes, we also get here the energy as well, what you can hear Yeah, data mine. And of course, you could also save this data into influx dB, you have to use the same function as before. So just process it in the right way can give you an example. So we are using here and function. And with this function, we are accessing all of the data like here. So I would like to have to the world digital data and this will be done in a new message. And with this message, we can also various our influx dBm is or influx dBm. And now we could say you're not the measurement is not done. It's the shelleyan Turn it on, then let's see if the values are inside our influx dB. Here we have the admin false password node red cruise. And it's called pixel Eddie I think yes. Then we go on no reds, then it should be Shelly. There we go. All of the things what we want to have here and submit. And we have here, for example, in micro amps, see the right things perfectly. Now we're getting the current data inside our influx dB.

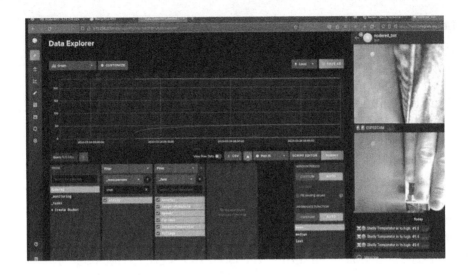

And with this triggering mechanism, we could say we want all of our information. And of course you could also adhere and time limit as well. For example, if you're not wants to have here 24/7 getting the data here you're adding in function. So that means that the triggering will only invoked in a certain specific time. Therefore, for example, you could set here and current timestamp. And I would like to have here, the current date and then also the current hour The current hour is detail to get hours I think it's called then could say if the hour is greater than five o'clock and the hour is under 23 Because afterwards it's not healthy to work anymore return the message and afterwards not so that means for example now we are getting all of these messages let's see. Perfect and now we are in the morning hours so I say after greater than 10 and 10 We should not get here anything out of it. So let's see because then I could do here and there's no one outside hours Deepak so this thing will be triggered and also we are getting back something from our Shelley but we are not triggered so we are not really triggering it to the Shelly as you can see here so it says spent with network traffic as well. And also we don't need in so much energy when we are not really working inside our office just just as an example so that we don't spam our database fool with nonsense data

# ESP8266 VS ESP32 XIAO

In this violin part I have two ESPs. And I would like to compare both approaches and will tell you the main main advantages and disadvantages of both of them. So here we have an d 182 66. And I have here and shield and battery shield where we can easily plug in the LiPo battery. And normally this LiPo battery, as you can see a 3.7 volts up to 4.2 world when it's fully charged, and this is too high to put it on the three world and also too low for the five folds and therefore we have to use such a shield to boost the voltage up to five world and then we can power those ESP. And also with the shield we can charge the LiPo battery later on. With this button, we can then re for example, here we have the wrist reset pin, we can from the deep sleep waking up the USB and with these patterns.

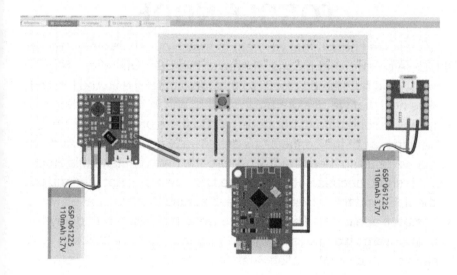

On the other hand, here we have the seeds to do the channel and this have this board has an onboard Pinna for the battery. So as you can see here on the backside of this small device we have two battery blots, plus and minus on with these two, we can directly access the battery and we can charge it with the USBC and that's really comfortable way and therefore we don't need anything else. And what we can see here we have a lot of power loss because first of all we have here and second board which has LEDs on it. Then a second we also have here an booster that means there's also some power loss implicit and therefore the efficiency of this schematic is not as high as we have it here because here we can directly charge it and also on the good thing is if you power here, the event battery is connected to the ESP board and we plug and play here the USB port then the sketch is not starting all over again. Because this is recognized and only the battery is charging. Really cool concept, especially when it comes to lipo.

# IOTBUTTON SKETCH AND TOGGLE NODE

The main task now is that we want to switch our shellye device with this OTA button. That means whenever this EOB UD button starts, it should send here an on or off, so that we can toggle it. And the first task is now that we use our basic sketch, and in this basic sketch, we want to send data to our node ret. So therefore, we have here all of thing, all of the connections are already implemented. And when we're using them the deep sleep, be aware to take this time not too short, because otherwise the USB device is not recognized in the IDE. And this is really tedious, because then you have always to restart it again, etc. Therefore, we work in a debug with delays, and afterwards we are using the deep sleep. So I would like to make your and client publish, then for example, you do all we can only say your team. But then from the button does matter, it should just trigger here something, then we have a delay. And then we have our deep sleep setting, the deep sleep setting. Let me see and what do we have here? Is this one, not? Not at all. Here we go. And we make en su print line going to sleep. And afterwards, the USB is starting all over again. So this is the first thing but we are not sending them to deep sleep. We are just saying yes. With make here and delay from around about 10 seconds, and then we see ESP restart. That's our testing device. So looks looking good.

Perfect, then we are switching back a copy this one to node red creating a new flow for example IoT button and then from the smart plugs I copy here the section not not the section, where is it? I would like to have the on off here to twitch this one implemented here because I would like to switch here there shall be device then I need the n m Qt Diem and M Quiddity.

In in Deepak and toggle toggle device if you don't have to toggle you can install it on the the node reds installation, and I think it should be toggle. Yes not read contributed toggle. So let's ask check what does this toggle Zack and M could add in will be the IoT button. Song then I would like to have here the toggling. So whenever the flow hits there, the toggling the toggle should have here. Two values. And Boolean true on Boolean false toggle value should be any except on and off and path through No. So let's see if it works. Normally when we are now triggering that flow, we're getting a true and we're getting a false true for us like we do it in a normal switch. And this is exactly what we have here. So here we manually can switch the Shelly as we did in the last section. True false. And now I also can do this with example here this one so let's do it a little bit in this side. Then I could say on off, on and off. So this is what we are now doing with the UT a button. That means whenever we are sending you a message to our flow, it will turn on or turned off. So here I have I think something in yes the topic after I have to do Get rid of it. So on finish false. Now it should work properly.

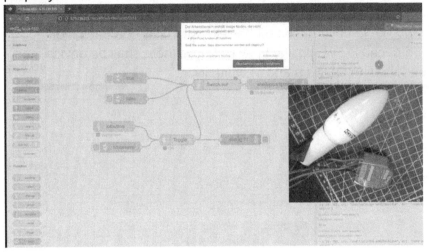

Now it's on. I have to deploy it. And now it's on. Now it's on 123 and dies off. Okay, now it's time to upload the sketch to our ESP. So and the thing is uploading. It was not right, sir. And now let's see here in the terminal. Or is it? If we have here any, I have 20 seconds, it needs a little bit time. So for the debugging purpose, we could use your only five seconds for example. So let's see, we got here a message, and it's on. And when I'm restarting now, the whole thing, let's restart it, or no, we have here and delay from 10 seconds. Here we can see it restarted. It's connected. It waits. 20 seconds for the next round. And then it should be toggled off. Let's see. It's nice on and now it's off. Perfect. This is exactly what we want. And so now we can use here, this toggle button for our IoT devices.

# 3D PRINT AND CALCULATION BATTERY CONSUMPTION

I created an small 3d printing housing. And as you can see here, here is an LiPo battery with 350 milliamps per hours. And I have to be careful because when I'm triggering here, this button, all of my power supply from the whole office will be shut down. Because the Shelly is switching off the socket. Here is the antenna, the external antenna, and this small reset button I installed here and normal push button parallel to this divan to small button. So this small button fits perfectly in the height with this casing. And with this housing, I can easily upload the sketch and also I can easily charge the device with this USB seal, then yours in small lit with a click. And this is now my ut button. And you can take it with you. And as we've seen before, it's an absolutely amazing runtime. So let's switch to the desktop. Severe and quick calculation with the seed studio I measured 60 milliamps in the new in the normal wakeup phase, that's 60 million barrels for 40 seconds. This is round about 2400 milliamps per seconds during the deep sleep. And I say here that the whole day it's in deep sleep because I only need it twice per day.

|  | Seeedstudio XIAO ESP32C3 | | |
|  | mA | seconds | mAs |
| During wake up | 60,00 | 40,00 | 2.400,00 |
| During deep sleep | 0,04 | 86.360,00 | 3.713,48 |
|  |  |  | 6.113,48 |
|  |  |  | 1,70 mAh / Tag |
|  |  | mAh |  |
|  | Battery Capacity | 320,00 |  |
|  | 60 % Nutzbar | 192,00 |  |
|  | Tage | 113,06 |  |

So 20 seconds uptime per day one for switching ons one for switching off. That means we have here in summary 9100 and certain milliamps per second, the battery capacity I think, or I assume that we only can use your 60% Of course of discharging and all of the other power loss. So in connection with our milliamps of power consumption per day, we can say for round about 100 days, we can have these battery life during the setup. And this is amazing because only each three months we have to charge it and this is also a real life example. So I only recharge it every two or three months this button and therefore it's really cool usage.

# INTERNET RADIO WIRING

Let's start with the worrying part. I have an ESP 32 developing port, here is the max 983578 amplifier, and it's called E squared s not seen. And here is an five watt speaker. So what you need is in ground and VCC, three world, then the TIN will as a data line goes to 20 GPIO 22, I think, then we have here at IBC K as the orange line goes to 26 and we have here to 25 the LRC channel and to plus and minus to the loudspeaker to the speaker itself.

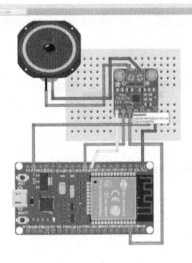

And those three GPIOs will later also defined in this sketch, but that's it. That's all what we need so far. So let's see here. Here is my smaller version of the ESB but you can use this also on the developing point, the E squared s module and here and small speaker just for the purpose. It's enough be aware when you use bigger speaker than you have also adhere an external power supply and not do everything on the internal GPOs because then you can break you developing bots

# INCLUDE LIBRARIES

The first thing is that we are now taking care of all of the dependencies and libraries what we need. Therefore we are only needing here the Pub Sub client, but I leave the analog right as well here inside. Then in the main cpp, there's a reference to our source. It's called from shapefile. ESP 32. Audio is credits. And this is an amazing it's an amazing library.

And here we are ESP 32. When we go to the source folder, we are downloading all of the content. I skipped the Opus decoder because I don't need it. But the AAC FLAC and mp3 folder and those two files, you take this, all of the files and including that into your source

folder. As you can see, here's the folder AAC was the decoder, CPP and the decoder H and the same with FLAC and mp3 and CPP and h then we are including the audio dot h in our basic sketch, the rest keeps the same and then we click on compile and then we can check if everything works as expected. And as we can see, we use a lot of our flash memory, but it successfully compiles and we know that the libraries are inside our sketch and works properly

# INTERNET RADIO STATIONS

Now let us start to implement the radial function of our sketch. And therefore we start at the beginning. And we are including here, the reference for the pins. So define the squared as connection. So we're making a define for E squared, S, D out, it's 20 tune. And also I have here for bclk and LRC, then we are creating the audio object. Simple as it is, we call it audio. And we are using this object later on for everything what we want to control. Now in our setup, we have here our connections. And now we are setting here, the pins with set pin out I think, yes, then we have here at the first is the B LCK, as you can see, and it's squared s bclk. And then the second parameter is the LRC, e squared s LRC. And then we have the D OD, e squared, S, D out. Very good, then we are setting the volume. I think it's from one, zero to 100. Let's see Set volume. He was this auto implementation, it's very cool. I set it to 10.

```
26 #define I2S_LRC 25
27
28 // create audio object
29 Audio audio;
30
31 void setup()
32 {                    connecttoFS
33   Serial.beg   connecttohost
34                connecttomarytts
35   connectAP(   connecttoSD
36   client.set   connecttospeech
37   client.set   setConnectionTimeout
38            CODEC_NONE
39   audio.setP   m_contentlength
40   //0-100    m_f_continue
41   audio.setV   parseContentType
42            m_controlCounter
43   //radio st   m_playlistContent
44   audio.conn
45   }
46
```

```
bool Audio::connectt'
oFS(fs::FS &fs, cons
t char *path, uint32
  t resumeFilePos = 0
))

Datei: Audio.h
```

And now the radio station, the radio station, we could do with audio connect to host, but it was too fast. Connect to host. And he comes to ul. And where do you get it, there are different examples. Let's see here. In the examples, for example, shopping back to the main example, only a little bit down and here we have different kind of radio stations what we can use, I have already prepared one in my area. And it's called coordinates and Austrian radio station. And that's it. That's what we want to have for the basic in the loop. We want to add the audio object and the loop the audio. And we have a lot of helper function, I copy all of this helper function these optional functions to my sketch as well. At the very end, then let's test if the compiler gives us a green light. And then we are uploading the sketch. And we have to have also a good Wi Fi connection because otherwise it puffer too much. So let's see him now the sketch should be started. And we use some music from an internet station and the good thing is, we're out here as you can see with this helper function. We get a lot of information out of it. But yeah, I'm gonna hit it works

# CONTROL RADIO VIA MQTT

Wouldn't it be nice that we can control our radio station via equity team and this is what we are wants to do now therefore we have a new flow. I have here two let's input here three in check notes. Then we have to M crudity arts. And I would like to control you, for example, the pause and resume I called topic in it. Or let's call it the radio slash pause, resume, zero false. And here the topic could be the radio sets while young. Then we have Yes, zero and false. Now we can connect here just by put on just by triggering. And I would like to have here for example, in number it doesn't matter because it it gets casted to a string. And to number for example, let's take 15 So this looks very good. So we click on deploy. And in our sketch Now we jump to the Wi Fi and crudity and nothing new for us. We jump up to the reconnect.

```
16  extern Audio audio;
17
18  void reconnect()
19  {
20    while (!client.connected())
21    {
22      Serial.print("Attempting MQTT connection...");
23      // Attempt to connect
24      clientId += String(random(0xffff), HEX);
25      if (client.connect(clientId                    ssword))
26      {                              boolean subscribe(const
27        Serial.println("connected 1/2 char *topic)
28        client.subscribe("iradio/")
29      }
30      else
31      {
32        Serial.print("failed, rc=");
33        Serial.print(client.state());
34        Serial.println(" try again in 5 seconds");
35        // Wait 5 seconds before retrying
36        delay(5000);
37      }
```

And we subscribe to client that subscribe. Radio, it's called pause, resume, copy, and in Edge radio set volume. Then, we want to capture the topic. So it's called you radio. pause, resume. And the same with said William with elsif. Set volume. When we got here, the pause and resume thing. It's easy for us because then we can just add here audio dot pause, resume, the function we call it. And that's it. So why is it possible to get we can access your audio object inside the Wi Fi M quality and because we have no Global's on our external reference, that's the reason because we include the audio dot h before the Wi Fi and quality and that means at the runtime, the Wi Fi and quality comes later. And then the audio dot h is already existing. If you get an error, you could make your own global state H as we did before, or you can use an external statement as well. Yeah, then I would also like you and Serial print line. And for example, we could see your audio dot get to read in title. So we have also access to that. Yeah, and to the volume. It's also easy, we could say audio that set volume, I call the topic as the function. And now we are transmitting the message 10 Because this is what we get transmitted over encoded in. But this isn't string, so be aware we have to cast it to an integer. And that's it. That's all what we want to do now. So let's test if the compiler has here any errors for us. Looking good so far. We're jumping back to the main and I go down to the helper function. So I called just one in the wifey and credit team. And wouldn't it be nice to get also the title. So let's see there should be anywhere here is the title. So, we can hear also sent clients publish the title, so II radio stream title. So, whenever the minute radio recognized and new title, we can get it then directly by M Quiddity. So we are not finished yet we have to also transmit the inform. This is the streaming inflam And now it should work.

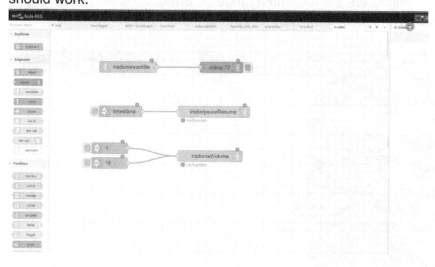

211

So before we upload here the sketch we have to also create the note you're in Node red, therefore we add in here an M could D in it And we could say here for example, it's radio string title serum then we get in here and Deepak and then we are ready to go on so we are switching back and uploading here our sketch. So the sketch is now on and now as you can hear it so I do the Learn the speaker a little bit nearer to the microphone. Then we want to pause it here we go, we just got the timestamp we resume, pause, pursue then set volume to 150 then I would like to have you just eight notes eight, here we getting back the title of the streaming title. And that's everything what we wanted and now we can control our innate radio like and Sonos or etc. With I'm crediting them with a dashboard or with not read

# SETTING THE ALARM TIME AND DASHBOARD

And of course you can create here and dashboard as well. So I've added here and button for on and off. And slider for the volume you can enter here the maximum range be aware 25 is really loud and I media, just half of the size for both of them.

And also I'm wants to have the stream title. So you the blackhead piece is now on. So let's turn it on, use the slider. And as you can see, we getting each each relia I have to start over again because it works better. So this is with the dashboards, you can control it also where you want. But also I would like to show you in the timestamp function here and repetition. We could for example also say between some or a daily daily point so we can make here an alarm clock for example. If you're standing up at six o'clock in the morning, from Monday to Friday, for example, and then you can waking up with the local radio. And so you have imitated a Sonos a box for example, which has all the same controls and also the same internet IoT connection, as we have fit here.

# DYNDNS AND CERTBOT

In this chapter, I would like to show you how you can use the Let's Encrypt chain of trust for your certificate. Let's Encrypt is an I think it's a nonprofit organization. And it's an area it's a nonprofit organization. And it's gives you the opportunity for an free SSL or TLS. Certificate, what we are simply used was our reverse proxy. But we are not using traffic for decrypting and encrypting our encoded communication. Because this is not too complicated. But it would go beyond the scope of this course. And therefore, I would like to focus on an easy version where you can use your SSL certificate also within Docker, and therefore, I'm already connected here to my server. And I've been here in my mosquito folder, so we already installed it in user local s bin mosquito. And this is the structure what we have with the config data, the lock and the password. Nothing new so far, what I would like to do now is I would like to have a new entry for our DNS, therefore I delete one of my DNS entries, because we need an a new one and we're creating here a new one, for example, it's called M crudity with SSL, very creative, I would say.

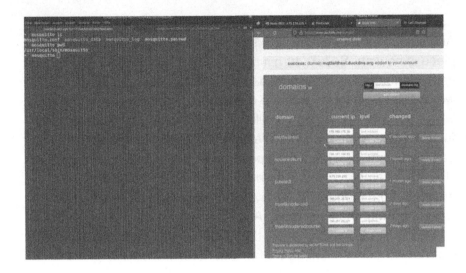

But now we have here a new entry and then let me see my IP address. Here we go. Then we update the IP address. And this is now the URL what we are using for our SSL certificate. And therefore that we can get it directly on our host system, we have to install the cert bot and cert bot will make the whole certificate thing is the reverse reverse proxy did but now we have to update at first so that we get your all of our necessary updates from the file system. Then we're making an NS install snipped dia, I have already installed it. So sudo apt install Snap again. And that is already in the newest version, then sudo snap install snap minus store. There we go on. And when the store is also installed, we could install now with sudo snap install minus minus classic cert bots, because this is what we need. So in my case, it's already installed. And now we can focus on acquiring a new certificate. And therefore we're typing in sudo cert bot cert only minus minus standalone minus minus preferred challenges HTT pn minus d. And now we have to add our new DNS or subdomain encoded here with S S L dot duck D and S dot O R G. And so now Certbot will acquire a year a new certificate for this URL.

And that's it. Normally, you have to enter here a few things. So for example, your email address, and I would and also you have to agree on the term of licenses, etc. And you should insert your real email address because the certificate is only valid as you can see here for three months. And if something and also here's the these files will be updated when the certificate renews. But surprised has set up a scheduled task to automatically renew but often or maybe it could be happening that the circuit doesn't renew it automatically. And then you're getting an email from Let's Encrypt that your certificate will be run out of time and that you have to renew it and then you can renewed with the search button. But here it's a no brainer. Just install cert bot and then we have now our encoded with is SSL dot duck DNS dot orgy with an SSL but it doesn't work because it's on the port 18 in the normal way and therefore in the next.

# MOUNT CERT FILES IN DOCKER

The first step now is that we are want to mount all of the certificate files into our mosquito Docker container. And here I'm already inside

215

the folder and so it's etc. Let's Encrypt life. And I fear a few other certificates as well for another example. But I would like to use now the M quality with ssl.or a gem. That's the files, what I would like to have now in my container, and I would like to have to serve the fortune in the private key. So are we doing this step by step. And therefore, I'm here in the user, local SP mosquito, where all of my Docker container files are. And I'm creating here a new folder, it's called Source, for example, we're jumping into certs. And now we are copying each file by the time and where do you get the file location, we got it from cert bot, before there gives you the exact location where it's saved. So etc, Let's Encrypt with the Tab key you can autocomplete it, then life encoded to you with SSL doc. And the first thing is this cert PM, and it should be called the same. So let's see if there is something inside Yes, then upper key and add a public key. And now I would like to have the full chain.

And I call it the same. But with the same name. Team full chain. There we go. And as the last one, we want to have the private key. So you also can see what's inside here to the private key and there we go. Now we have here all of the files. So let's see what is the you can see it's only restrict restricted access. But I think there is some problem with the ownership. Because you can remember, we have changed the ownership to the use of 1883. So therefore, I would like to change it. Record C for all files 132 The whole folder of certs. So let's jump into certs. Let's see if it changed. There we go. If we have 10 later on problems with permissions, then we have to change also the settings but I think it should work. Okay, so far, so good. Now we have already created a folder. And what we do now is we are killing the existing container. And we want to create a new one. And now I've prepared the docker run statement and edit two lines. The first line what I added is the 9001 I is now the 8883 this is the standard port for TLS communication with mosquito and I've added here and second our fifth volume and this is where the certs are located. This is the file location on our host system and this is the inside the container. So enter and I would like I would say let's check if the files are in the container. Therefore we say Docker exec DIR for interactive, then the name from the container it's mosquito server. Here we go. And sh for Shell. Then we are inside the container we have mounted it in the mosquito inserts and there we go. We have here the photos and we can also access it full chain and tailor the price care perfect exit and with jumping out of the container and this is the first step what we want to prepare defassa inside the container

# MOSQUITTO.CONF AND NODERED BROKER SETTINGS

The next step is that we have to edit our configuration file so that all of the changes are taking into the production system. Therefore, we open here, the mosquito config file. And I've already prepared here four lines. So now we have also to listen to 883, you can also leave these file onto your system because maybe there are some devices, which are not using SSL or TLS. And therefore, you can use both of them because you already don't let any external access to your system. So why not using both of them, but you should prefer here those TLS connections, then we are referenced the cert file is now under mosquito cert cert PM, see a file and the key file. Now we are saving this file. And we can restart your our system.

And now the first check is if you can enter the Docker container, then the mosquito configuration file could find all of the cert files. If you get here and restart Iran, then it might be that some of you mosquito configuration is broken. Because in the mosquito log, you don't find really any information regarding this. Maybe you see in the mosquito log something like it's not found on the file system, etc. But this gives an indication that there is something wrong with the source virus. So therefore, I can jump up. No, we're jumping in to our mosquito server because I would like to test it now in our node, right. So this is my reconnection error. So now I would like to have here and Quiddity in our next one and one debug. And then we have here the normal SSL. So without SSL. And here we have with SSL make any connection. And now with SSL, we have to add here and new program. The new broker is now as we call it here, it's the M Quiddity with SSL. So this is our new host, SS I duck DNS Orci, the port is 8883. We are now using TLS jumping into TLS configuration.

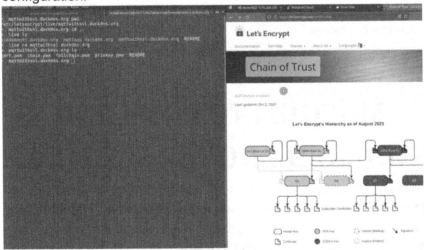

And here we have our certificate, you could also upload the CA certificate but it's not necessary. The CA certificate is under this URL. And then you can download for example here the PEM file for self signed. But normally, all of the software has the certificate from Let's Encrypt already implemented. Therefore we're clicking here and adding here those one finish then deploying, deploying. And let's see I've forgotten something because we already also have here some security things so it's called pics lady in red. safe finish deploying. And now we are connected with both of them. And this is what I would like to desktop. So I'm here in the container. Now I can use here on mosquito Publish. And first of all, I'm using the localhost, the topic is without SSL, the message is I am not encrypted. And I have to adhere the user and the password within Pn is thought it's called now alright. So let's see if this works. I'm not encrypted with our SSL. And now with the SSL I don't need your any links to one certificate. So therefore I say mosquito pup H and it's called T naught m could it do without SSL L dot duck DNS or GM? The topic is with SSL messages. I am encrypted yay. Uses pixel ad password is no Red Cross, enter. Unable to connect, so let's see what is my error and as always spelling errors, your equity with not without SSL with SSL. And now I'm getting here I'm encrypted on this topic and this broker settings on this port and we are having an encrypted communication with M Quiddity. And that's the part what we already mentioned here so we can change here on the settings also here in the note read the broker settings and quality without the SSL topic and then we are ready to go with our SSL certificate.

# ESP32 AND MQTT WITH TLS

And now we want to edit also our basic Wi Fi sketch so that we can use here the TLS, also with our ESP, and therefore we have to edit here a little bit of a few things. Therefore, we are jumping into Wi Fi equity team going to the top. And the first thing what we are needing to do with CR to change the includes to on Wi Fi client secure.

Then we have here and certificate, the route car from Let's Encrypt, maybe it will work also without it, but I've used it so you can copy and paste it from him. You can find it under the Let's Encrypt certificates. Here you go on, then you have the PEM, for example. It's and file and text file. So you can open this PEM file by drag and drop it only to an text editor. And then you can copy and paste all of this content to you ESPN. Therefore, we switch back. So as you can see, this is exactly the thing. And now we have to prepare for the ESP that means we need here such quotes. And at the end when making a linebreak. Next quote, and backslash. And also you call it Let's Encrypt for example root CA and that's it, then we have to change the server address. It's not the IP, it's now the DNS with the same use and password. And then what we have to change also is let me see in the main No, where is it? Ciao here, we have the Wi Fi client secure that was before, not what the client the security trust the Wi Fi client. And this will be now handed to the Pub Sub client. And in the main we have now the ESP client we have to set here the CA certificate.

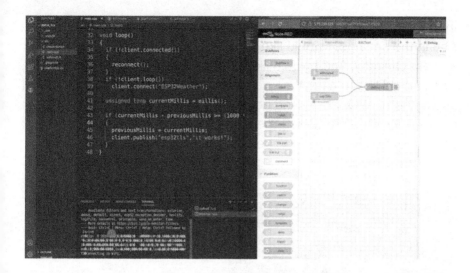

That's the certificate from here what we end the TM and then the encoded the server but with the port 8883 Then the callback as we did before and now we can publish here for example, ESP 32 TLS and it works and our node read I've changed here the topic as well so now I'm connecting the ESP then let's open here and restarted let's see if the connection is made connecting to Wi Fi and here we got already two of the things so restarted again. Can't get em Wi Fi connection, attempting encoded a connection. And every three seconds we should get here and message. Perfect. Oh I have no zero print. So we only see it here. And this is now with an encrypted version to our mosquito broker from the ESPN to node red to mosquito

# ANALYZE MQTT TRAFFIC WITH WIRESHARK

Let's observe and monitor our own encoded D things. And therefore, I would like to start your Wireshark. I'm sure all of you already know what Wireshark is, it's in software where we can analyze our traffic. And therefore, I would like to catch any of the traffic. And as you can see, I use ETS on the local machine is root, then we start here on observing, then we can go to the settings. And in the settings, I would like to go to protocols to MQ TT. Let's see em Quiddity. And I would like to see show messages as text. And I would like to have the encrypted one. Okay. And then I'm seeing here, m Quiddity. And nothing happened so far. So I'm creating a new window, and then on my local machine and not on the server because I have to be in the exactly in the same network, as we have here.

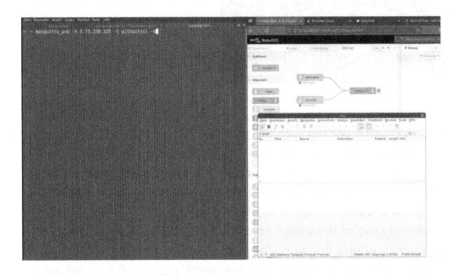

So I've installed here also the mosquito client for publishing something, then the local host is known the IP address from my server, the topic is without SSL, and the message is, can wire shark see that message and also my username and password then have grabbed the user is pixel ID and the password is no dreads. So then, let's see what happens. So I've entered now with my local machine, those message we see using Connect command so it's also in connection acknowledge, then we see and publish message then let's make this a little bit bigger. You will have the message in clear form can Wireshark see that message and also my username. And with this acknowledged that was it in the command also in the Connect command I can see here, the pixel Edie and Don node red course 2023 And here's the password. And here's the username as well. And this was just a short demonstration that you can also observe with Wireshark here you and quality traffic and also can

observe what is going on directly on the server and what is
encrypted and not .

Made in the USA
Monee, IL
03 December 2023

48092370R10122